Volume Three: Materia Materia of Homeopathic Gemstones

Dr Víctor Denis Purcell

Published by Dr Víctor Denis Purcell, 2024.

VOLUME THREE: MATERIA MATERIA OF HOMEOPATHIC GEMSTONES

First edition. July 28, 2024.

Copyright © 2024 Dr Víctor Denis Purcell.

ISBN: 979-8227300461

Written by Dr Víctor Denis Purcell.

Dedication: Tayler, Matt and Marco and Alexander

Volume Three

Materia Medica of Homeopathic Gemstones

Chapter Listing:

- **Chapter 1:introduction to homeopathic medicine**

- **Chapter 2: Materia Medica**

Disclaimer ◈

Please read the following terms and conditions carefully before proceeding.

General Information Purposes Only: The information provided in the following is for general information and entertainment purposes only. All information is provided in good faith; however, the author makes no representation or warranty of any kind, express or implied, regarding the accuracy, adequacy, validity, reliability, availability, or completeness of any information on the following.

Not Medical Advice: The content provided below is not intended to be a substitute for professional medical advice, diagnosis, or treatment. Always seek the advice of your physician or other qualified health providers with any questions you may have regarding a medical condition or health concerns.

No Doctor-Patient Relationship: reading the information below does not constitute establishing a doctor-patient relationship. Any health information communicated is not an endorsement, diagnosis, or treatment regimen.

Professional Assistance: You must not rely on the information below as an alternative to medical advice from your doctor or other professional healthcare providers. If you believe you are experiencing any medical condition, seek immediate medical attention from a licensed healthcare provider.

Risks of Self-Diagnosis: Self-diagnosis can lead to harm, and healthcare professionals must perform diagnosis and treatment.

Limitation of Warranties: The medical information provided is "as is" without any representations or warranties, express or implied. The author makes no representations or warranties concerning the medical report.

Liability: You agree to release the author from all liability and to hold him harmless from any legal claims related to the medical information provided.

Contact a doctor: Do not disregard, avoid, or delay obtaining medical advice from a qualified healthcare provider because of something you may have read in this book or below.

You do understand and agree to the terms of this disclaimer. If you do not agree with these terms, you are not authorized to obtain information from or otherwise proceed.

- **Chapter 1, introduction to homeopathic medicine**

In the realm of medical sciences, where evidence-based practices and biochemical interventions dominate the landscape, there exists a field that takes a markedly different approach: homeopathic medicine. This discipline, rooted in the late 18th century, was pioneered by Samuel Hahnemann, a German physician disillusioned by the prevailing medical practices of his time. Homeopathy is founded on principles that challenge conventional medical paradigms, particularly the notions of dosage, symptom treatment, and the nature of healing itself.

This chapter seeks to provide an in-depth introduction to the foundational principles, history, and philosophy that constitute the backbone of homeopathic medicine. By delving into the core concepts of "similia similibus curentur" (like cures like) and the use of highly diluted remedies, it aims to shed light on how homeopathy stimulates the body's intrinsic healing responses. The journey begins with an exploration of the rich historical roots of homeopathy, from its inception by Hahnemann to the evolution and adaptation of his principles over time. Understanding this historical context is crucial, as it reveals the motivations and insights that drove Hahnemann to develop a system of medicine that emphasized gentle, individualized care over the often harsh and invasive treatments of his era.

Central to this discussion is the Law of Similars, which posits that substances capable of producing symptoms in healthy individuals can be used to treat similar symptoms in the sick. This principle was a radical departure from the conventional medical practices of Hahnemann's time and continues to be a cornerstone of homeopathic practice. Through meticulous experimentation and documentation, Hahnemann developed a comprehensive materia medica that guides homeopaths in matching patient symptoms with appropriate remedies.

Another key aspect of homeopathy covered in this chapter is the process of potentization and succussion, methods developed by Hahnemann to prepare remedies in a way that enhances their healing properties while minimizing toxicity. This process of serial dilution and vigorous shaking, which imprints the "memory" of the original substance onto the diluent, challenges conventional pharmacological beliefs but remains a fundamental practice in homeopathic medicine.

The chapter also delves into the principle of the minimum dose, which emphasizes using the smallest possible amount of a substance to stimulate a healing response. This approach aims to avoid side effects and supports the body's natural healing processes without overwhelming them. It reflects a broader philosophical stance within homeopathy that respects the body's inherent wisdom and capacity for self-healing.

Furthermore, this chapter highlights the individualized approach of homeopathic treatment. Unlike the standardized protocols of conventional medicine, homeopathy tailors its remedies to the unique physical, emotional, and mental symptoms of each patient. This personalized care extends to chronic and complex conditions, emphasizing a holistic view of health that integrates mental, emotional, and physical well-being.

The concept of vital force, or vital energy, is also examined. This vitalist perspective views health as a state of dynamic equilibrium maintained by an intrinsic energy force, which, when imbalanced, leads to disease. Homeopathic remedies aim to restore balance to this vital force, a concept that aligns with various traditional healing systems around the world.

Lastly, the chapter addresses the Doctrine of Drug Proving, a method by which homeopaths determine the effects of remedies through systematic testing on healthy individuals. This empirical approach ensures that the therapeutic application of remedies is grounded in direct human experience, emphasizing the importance of subjective reports as valuable diagnostic tools.

This chapter provides a comprehensive overview of homeopathy's unique approach to medicine, one that emphasizes gentle, individualized care, the use of minimal doses, and a holistic view of health. By understanding these principles and their historical development, readers will gain insight into the distinct nature of homeopathic practice and its enduring relevance in the broader field of healthcare.

- **Main content:**

As we have seen in the above, in this chapter, we delve into the fundamental principles, history, and philosophy underpinning homeopathic medicine. We explore the core concepts of "similia similibus curentur" (like cures like) and the utilization of highly diluted remedies to stimulate the body's intrinsic healing mechanisms. Additionally, we trace the historical origins of homeopathy, from its inception by Samuel Hahnemann to the evolution and development of his principles. This foundational understanding will provide readers with a comprehensive overview of this distinct form of medicine.

The Genesis of Homeopathy: Samuel Hahnemann's Vision

The genesis of homeopathy is rooted in the work of Samuel Hahnemann, an 18th-century German physician. Disenchanted with the medical practices of his time—often characterized by harsh and ineffective treatments—Hahnemann sought a more humane and rational approach to healing. His pursuit led to the principle of "similia similibus curentur" or "like cures like," which became the cornerstone of homeopathic medicine. This principle marked a significant departure from the prevailing medical practices of bloodletting, purging, and the use of toxic substances. Hahnemann envisioned a medical system that supported the body's natural healing tendencies, a concept he found echoed in ancient texts but not rigorously applied in a systematic medical framework.

Hahnemann's early life and education were instrumental in shaping his medical philosophy. Born in 1755 in Meissen, Germany, he exhibited a keen intellect and a passion for learning. He studied medicine at the University of Leipzig and later at the University of Erlangen, where he was awarded his MD. His dissatisfaction with the crude and often harmful medical practices of his time drove him to seek alternatives. His profound knowledge of chemistry, pharmacology, and various languages allowed him to access a broad range of medical texts, further fueling his quest for a better healing system.

The Law of Similars: Understanding "Like Cures Like"

The foundational principle of homeopathy, "like cures like," posits that substances capable of causing disease symptoms in healthy individuals can treat similar symptoms in the sick. Hahnemann's discovery was catalyzed by his observation of the effects of cinchona bark (quinine) in treating malaria, noting that it produced malaria-like symptoms in healthy individuals. This observation led to further experimentation and the formulation of a doctrine suggesting that substances inducing symptoms in healthy individuals could be used to stimulate the body's healing processes. This law signified a profound interconnectedness between humans and nature, which homeopathy seeks to harness.

As Hahnemann continued his experiments, he documented the specific effects of various substances on healthy individuals, a process termed "provings." Volunteers, including Hahnemann himself, would ingest a substance and meticulously record the resulting physical, emotional, and mental symptoms. These observations formed the rudimentary materia medica of homeopathy, guiding the selection of remedies to match a patient's symptom profile.

Hahnemann further refined the preparation of homeopathic remedies through a method known as potentization, which involves systematic dilution and succussion (vigorous shaking) at each dilution step. He proposed that this process not only reduced the toxicity of the substance but also enhanced its therapeutic properties, even when diluted beyond the point of containing any molecules of the original substance. Hahnemann's work with provings extended over many years and involved a wide range of substances, including plants, minerals, and animal products. His dedication to rigorously testing these substances on himself and other volunteers provided a wealth of empirical data that formed the backbone of homeopathic practice.

Individualized treatment is another pivotal element of homeopathy. Unlike the one-size-fits-all approach of conventional medicine, homeopathy emphasizes the uniqueness of each patient's illness experience. Effective treatment requires a thorough understanding of the patient's symptoms, lifestyle, and psychological state, acknowledging the complexity of human health and tailoring remedies to the individual rather than the disease.

This holistic approach extends to the mental and emotional aspects of health. Hahnemann observed that emotional states such as grief or shock could significantly impact physical health, a perspective that was innovative for his time. Homeopathy views disease as a disturbance of the body's vital force, with remedies aiming to stimulate this vital energy to restore balance and health.

The practice of homeopathy spread as Hahnemann's students and followers continued to practice and teach his methods. By the early 19th century, homeopathy had taken root in Europe and America, offering a gentler alternative to the often harsh and invasive medical practices of the time. Hahnemann's meticulous documentation and the publication of his works, such as "The Organon of the Healing Art," played a crucial role in disseminating his ideas. The "Organon" outlined the principles of homeopathy and provided practical guidelines for its practice, becoming the foundational text for homeopathic practitioners.

The Art of Dilution: Potentization and Succussion

In homeopathy, potentization and succession are pivotal processes transforming substances into therapeutic agents. Potentization involves systematic dilution, often to a point where no molecules of the starting material are detectable, combined with succussion to transfer the substance's essence or 'energy' into the medium (water or alcohol). Hahnemann developed these methods to mitigate the toxic effects observed with undiluted substances, discovering that the curative properties persisted and were even enhanced through dilution and succussion.

This methodology challenges conventional pharmacology, which relies on dose-dependent effects. The theory behind potentization suggests that the process imprints the memory of the substance onto the diluent, interacting with the body's vital force. Each level of dilution, known as potency, is marked by a specific ratio, and the choice of potency is tailored to the individual patient based on their symptoms.

Succussion is believed to activate the medicinal properties of the solution. Despite skepticism from mainstream science regarding the mechanisms by which succussion enhances therapeutic efficacy, practitioners and patients attest to its qualitative difference, suggesting that shaking is integral to remedy preparation.

The concept of potentization extends beyond remedy preparation to reflect a broader holistic approach. It underscores that the remedy's effectiveness lies not only in its substance but also in its preparation and administration, emphasizing a process-oriented approach to healing. Hahnemann's theory of potentization was not static; he continued to refine and improve his methods throughout his life. His later works, such as the sixth edition of "The Organon," introduced the concept of using even higher dilutions (LM potencies), which he believed could achieve deeper and more lasting healing effects.

Potentization also embodies the homeopathic respect for the complexity and sensitivity of the body. It operates on the understanding that very subtle triggers can activate the body's healing mechanisms and that these mechanisms are capable of profound responses. The tailored potencies speak to this sensitivity, offering a spectrum of stimuli that can be matched to the individual's health and vitality.

The Principle of the Minimum Dose

The principle of the minimum dose in homeopathy posits that the lowest amount of a substance needed to initiate a healing response is the most desirable dosage. This principle aims to avoid side effects and supports the body's natural healing processes without overpowering or suppressing them. Hahnemann sought a gentle and respectful approach to healing, contrasting with the harsh methods of conventional treatments.

The minimum dose principle operates in tandem with potentization to produce remedies interacting with the body's vital force rather than directly affecting its physiology. The goal is to provide enough stimulus for the body's healing response without causing aggravation, reflecting a patient-centered approach that respects the body's pace and capacity for recovery.

Critics argue that minute doses, often beyond the presence of the original substance, cannot have any effect. However, homeopaths assert that clinical outcomes justify their approach, calling for an expanded understanding of drug action beyond material dose-response relationships.

The principle of the minimum dose also speaks to a philosophical stance recognizing the body as a self-healing organism, with medicine supporting rather than usurping the healing process. This principle remains a cornerstone of homeopathic medicine, emphasizing gentle intervention and respect for the body's inherent healing capabilities. The principle aligns with modern trends towards personalized medicine and the minimization of pharmacological interventions, reflecting a growing recognition of the need for more individualized and less invasive therapeutic approaches.

The Individualized Approach: The Patient as the Central Focus

The individualized approach in homeopathy views each patient as a unique entity requiring a tailored treatment strategy. Unlike the standardized protocols of conventional medicine, homeopathy emphasizes comprehensive assessment of the patient's physical, emotional, and mental symptoms, along with their medical history and life circumstances.

This approach demands thorough case-taking, with homeopaths conducting in-depth interviews to understand the patient's subtle symptoms and responses to various influences. The detailed questioning explores aspects such as food preferences, sleep patterns, and emotional temperament, which are crucial in selecting the most fitting remedy.

The individualized approach acknowledges the complexity of the human condition, respecting that the manifestations of illness are as diverse as the people experiencing them. Effective treatment must resonate with the patient's overall well-being, stimulating the body's healing processes in alignment with the individual's vitality and health.

Homeopaths view this approach to honor the whole person, addressing mental and emotional health as integral components of overall well-being. This dynamic process is responsive to changes in the patient's symptoms and health status, allowing for a flexible and evolving treatment strategy. This individualization extends to chronic conditions, where homeopaths may adjust remedies over time to reflect the shifting nature of the patient's health and circumstances.

Moreover, the individualized approach in homeopathy involves creating a therapeutic partnership between the practitioner and the patient. Homeopaths invest significant time in understanding the patient's life story, experiences, and personality traits, fostering a deeper connection that enhances the healing process. This relationship is built on trust, empathy, and mutual respect, providing a supportive environment for patients to engage actively in their healing journey.

The Holistic Philosophy: Treating the Whole Person

The holistic philosophy in homeopathy involves treating the individual in their entirety, considering the complex interplay between mind, body, and spirit. This approach views symptoms as expressions of the body's attempt to heal itself and emphasizes restoring balance within the whole person.

In practice, this philosophy involves meticulous consideration of the patient's physical symptoms, emotional state, mental health, and life circumstances. Homeopaths believe that emotional disturbances or life stressors can manifest as physical ailments, and vice versa, necessitating a comprehensive evaluation.

By addressing the person, homeopathy aims to bring about a state of harmony where health can flourish on all levels. Remedies are intended to support the body's self-healing mechanisms, encouraging a return to balance rather than merely suppressing symptoms.

The holistic approach extends to understanding and treating chronic illnesses, where symptoms can be complex and multifaceted. Homeopathy seeks to understand the underlying patterns of sustaining illness, working towards a sustainable and long-term restoration of health. This approach also involves preventative measures, promoting lifestyle changes that support overall well-being and reduce the likelihood of disease recurrence.

Homeopathy's holistic philosophy aligns with contemporary integrative medicine practices, which advocate for a comprehensive approach to health that includes diet, exercise, stress management, and mental health support. Homeopaths often provide guidance on these aspects, recognizing that a balanced lifestyle is crucial for maintaining health and preventing disease.

The Dynamis Concept: Vital Force as the Essence of Life

The concept of vital force, also known as vital energy, is fundamental to homeopathy's understanding of health and disease. It posits that a dynamic energy force animates all living beings, governing their physical functions and adaptive processes. When this vital force is imbalanced, it leads to symptoms of illness, and homeopathic remedies aim to stimulate this energy to restore balance.

This vitalist perspective differentiates homeopathy from conventional Western medicine, which is primarily mechanical and biochemical. Homeopaths assert that the vital force, although not directly observable, is discernible by its effects. The state of the vital force is reflected in the individual's overall well-being, including their mental, emotional, and physical conditions.

In practice, homeopaths seek to match the remedy's energy with the patient's disturbed vital force. This interaction is believed to stimulate the self-healing process. Symptoms are seen as expressions of a disturbed vital force, guiding the selection of an appropriate remedy to address the underlying imbalance.

The vital force concept is central to homeopathy's holistic treatment of patients, recognizing that symptoms indicate a more profound disturbance rather than merely organ dysfunction. It aligns with other traditional healing systems, such as qi in Traditional Chinese Medicine or prana in Ayurveda, emphasizing the balance of life energy for good health.

Various factors, including emotional states, environmental conditions, and lifestyle choices, influence the strength and harmony of the vital force. Therefore, a homeopath may guide diet, stress management, and other aspects of life that can support the patient's vitality. Maintaining a robust and balanced vital force is critical to resilience against illness.

In dealing with chronic diseases, the concept of the vital force is particularly significant. Homeopaths consider the long-term vitality and energy patterns of the individual, aiming to gradually restore the disturbed vital force to a state of equilibrium. Chronic symptoms indicate a deep-seated imbalance in the vital force that requires a sustained therapeutic strategy.

The vital force concept also informs the homeopathic perspective on prevention. A well-balanced vital energy confers immunity and resilience, reducing disease susceptibility. Thus, homeopathy places a strong emphasis on strengthening the vital force as a means of preventing illness and promoting long-term health.

The Principle of Potentization: Unlocking Remedial Energy

The principle of potentization is a hallmark of homeopathy, representing a unique process by which remedies are prepared to enhance their healing properties. This involves serial dilution and succussion (vigorous shaking) of a substance, aiming to release its energetic potential. Homeopaths believe this process amplifies the remedy's therapeutic qualities, stimulating the body's vital force while minimizing toxic side effects.

Potentization challenges conventional dose-response relationships, suggesting that the therapeutic qualities of a substance can operate at a level subtler than the molecular or chemical. The process is thought to imprint the substance's "memory" onto the diluent, with each dilution and succussion step increasing this energetic imprint.

The choice of potency is critical and tailored to each patient, considering factors such as sensitivity, illness nature, and symptom duration. The meticulous preparation of remedies reflects homeopathy's respect for both the material and non-material aspects of healing.

Potentization is not merely a means of remedy preparation but also a philosophical stance on the nature of medicine and healing. It posits that energy and information are central to health and that substances have capacities beyond their chemical composition. These principles challenge conventional medical paradigms and invite a broader understanding of what is therapeutically possible.

Homeopaths argue that potentization allows for a more precise and personalized approach to treatment. By selecting the appropriate potency, practitioners can tailor the remedy to the individual needs of the patient, ensuring that the treatment is both effective and gentle. This personalized approach is a testament to the detailed nature of homeopathic practice and its commitment to individualized care.

The Doctrine of Drug Proving: Understanding Remedies through Human Experience

The Doctrine of Drug Proving is fundamental to homeopathy, whereby substances are systematically tested on healthy individuals to determine the range of symptoms they produce. These symptoms are meticulously cataloged to create detailed remedy profiles, ensuring therapeutic applications are grounded in empirical observation and direct human experience.

Drug proving involves healthy volunteers taking a homeopathic potency of a substance and recording all changes experienced. These self-observations contribute to the homeopathic materia medica, guiding the selection of remedies to match patient symptoms.

The methodology emphasizes safety, with remedies used in highly diluted forms to minimize adverse effects. Drug proving reflects homeopathy's empirical approach, respecting the nuances of human experiences and emphasizing the importance of subjective reports as valuable diagnostic tools.

The records from drug provings are compiled and scrutinized by homeopaths to discern patterns and characteristic symptoms that are consistently produced by the substance. These typical symptoms become essential in the homeopathic prescription process as they guide the practitioner in matching a patient's symptoms with the remedy profile.

The Doctrine of Drug Proving is also a testament to the homeopathic respect for the subtlety of human perception and the complexity of human experiences. Unlike conventional trials that may dismiss subjective experiences as irrelevant or anecdotal, homeopathy values these personal reports as essential data for understanding the multi-dimensional impact of remedies.

Drug proving is an ongoing process, reflecting homeopathy's openness to discovering new remedies and expanding its materia medica. As society encounters new substances and our environments change, homeopathy recognizes the need to explore and understand the healing potential of new agents continuously.

Summary of this chapter

Homeopathic medicine represents a unique and distinct paradigm within the broader field of medical sciences, characterized by its foundational principles, historical context, and philosophical underpinnings. This summary provides a comprehensive overview of the salient features of homeopathy, reflecting its evolution and enduring relevance in contemporary healthcare.

Homeopathy originated in the late 18th century through the pioneering work of Samuel Hahnemann, a German physician who sought alternatives to the harsh and often ineffective medical practices of his time. Dissatisfied with conventional treatments such as bloodletting and purging, Hahnemann formulated the principle of "similia similibus curentur" or "like cures like." This doctrine posits that substances capable of producing symptoms in healthy individuals can be utilized to treat similar symptoms in the sick, thus stimulating the body's intrinsic healing mechanisms. This foundational concept marked a significant departure from the prevailing medical theories and practices, setting the stage for the development of a new therapeutic system.

Central to homeopathy is the process of potentization, which involves the serial dilution and succussion (vigorous shaking) of substances to enhance their therapeutic properties while minimizing toxicity. This method, which imprints the "memory" of the original substance onto the diluent, challenges conventional pharmacological principles. However, it remains a cornerstone of homeopathic practice, reflecting a nuanced understanding of the interplay between substance, energy, and the body's vital force.

The principle of the minimum dose further distinguishes homeopathy from conventional medicine. By advocating for the smallest possible amount of a substance to elicit a healing response, homeopathy emphasizes a gentle, patient-centered approach that avoids overwhelming the body's natural processes. This minimalistic strategy aligns with a broader philosophical stance that respects the body's inherent wisdom and self-regulatory capabilities.

Homeopathy's individualized approach to treatment underscores its commitment to personalized care. Unlike standardized protocols in conventional medicine, homeopathy tailors its remedies to the unique constellation of physical, emotional, and mental symptoms presented by each patient. This holistic perspective integrates various dimensions of health, recognizing the interconnectedness of the mind, body, and spirit. Such an approach is particularly valuable in managing chronic and complex conditions, where a deeper understanding of the patient's overall well-being is paramount.

The concept of vital force, or vital energy, is integral to homeopathy's theoretical framework. This vitalist perspective posits that health is maintained by a dynamic equilibrium of intrinsic energy, which, when disrupted, manifests as disease. Homeopathic remedies aim to restore balance to this vital force, a notion that resonates with various traditional healing systems worldwide, such as qi in Traditional Chinese Medicine and prana in Ayurveda.

The empirical basis of homeopathy is further reinforced by the Doctrine of Drug Proving. This methodology involves systematically testing substances on healthy individuals to document the full spectrum of symptoms they produce. These detailed observations form the materia medica, guiding practitioners in selecting remedies that match the patient's symptom profile. This rigorous, experiential approach underscores the importance of subjective reports as valuable diagnostic tools and ensures that homeopathic treatments are grounded in direct human experience.

In conclusion, homeopathic medicine offers a distinctive and holistic approach to healthcare, emphasizing individualized treatment, minimal dosing, and the restoration of vital force. Its principles challenge conventional medical paradigms, advocating for a patient-centered, gentle, and integrative approach to healing. By understanding these foundational concepts and their historical evolution, one gains a deeper appreciation of homeopathy's role and potential within the broader landscape of medical practice. This comprehensive overview underscores the enduring relevance and adaptability of homeopathic principles in addressing contemporary health challenges, reflecting a commitment to a more personalized and holistic vision of health and well-being.

Chapter 2: Materia Medica

Proustite: Comprehensive Guide on Spiritual and Physical Healing Properties

Overview

Proustite, known for its vibrant red to scarlet hues and striking crystal formations, is a rare and captivating crystal valued for its powerful energy and metaphysical properties. This gemstone is often associated with clarity and vitality. Proustite is celebrated for its ability to enhance intuition and promote overall well-being.

Spiritual and Psychic Benefits

Proustite is renowned for its ability to alleviate stress and anxiety. Its vibrant energy promotes a sense of peace and tranquility, helping to calm the mind and reduce emotional tension. This makes it an excellent companion for meditation and stress management practices.

Connected to the root and third eye chakras, Proustite enhances intuition and psychic abilities. It encourages deep spiritual insight and clarity, helping individuals to connect with their inner wisdom and higher consciousness.

Proustite is a stone of vitality and energy. It supports physical and emotional resilience, helping individuals to overcome fatigue and regain their strength.

Known for its ability to amplify healing energies, Proustite is used to enhance both personal energy and the effectiveness of other healing crystals. It is beneficial in promoting a balanced and harmonious energy flow during healing sessions.

Proustite aids in balancing the body's subtle energies. It aligns the chakras and stabilizes emotions, fostering a harmonious internal environment that supports spiritual and emotional well-being.

Utilized in various forms such as raw crystals, jewelry, and meditation tools, Proustite is a key component in holistic healing practices. It is often used in energy layouts to align and balance the body's energy centers.

Physical Healing Properties

Proustite is believed to boost physical vitality and energy levels. It helps to invigorate the body, enhancing stamina and overall health.

This crystal supports healthy blood circulation and detoxification. It helps to purify the blood and strengthen the cardiovascular system, contributing to overall vitality and well-being.

Proustite aids in detoxifying the body, supporting liver function and cleansing the system of toxins. This contributes to improved metabolic health and overall well-being.

Proustite supports the body's natural healing processes by promoting cellular regeneration. It aids in the recovery from injuries and illnesses, speeding up the healing process.

Proustite is believed to enhance the immune system, helping the body to fight off illnesses more effectively. It supports the body's natural defenses and promotes overall health and vitality.

Potential Homeopathic Uses

If Proustite were to be used as a homeopathic remedy, its indications might include:

Psychological Symptoms: Anxiety, emotional stress, and lack of clarity. It may also help in cases of emotional instability and spiritual confusion.

Physical Symptoms: Blood health issues, detoxification needs, and immune system deficiencies.

Behavioral Symptoms: Difficulty in coping with stress, lack of motivation, and a tendency towards emotional imbalance.

Proustite's homeopathic profile would focus on its ability to invigorate, protect, and rejuvenate, making it suitable for addressing conditions related to stress, blood health, and overall well-being.

Conclusion

Proustite is a vital crystal in holistic healing, celebrated for its vibrant beauty and versatile healing properties. Whether used for stress relief, intuitive enhancement, or as a revitalizing talisman, Proustite serves as a potent aid in achieving physical health and spiritual harmony. Like all alternative practices, these should be considered as complementary to conventional medical treatments.

Hematite: Comprehensive Guide on Spiritual and Physical Healing Properties

Overview

Hematite, known for its metallic sheen and grounding energy, is a powerful crystal valued for its stabilizing and protective properties. This gemstone is often associated with strength and clarity. Hematite is celebrated for its ability to enhance focus and promote overall well-being.

Spiritual and Psychic Benefits

Hematite is renowned for its ability to alleviate stress and anxiety. Its grounding energy promotes a sense of stability and calm, helping to clear the mind and reduce emotional tension. This makes it an excellent companion for meditation and stress management practices.

Connected to the root chakra, Hematite enhances grounding and protection. It encourages a strong connection to the earth, helping individuals to feel secure and centered.

Hematite is a stone of mental clarity and focus. It supports clear thinking and decision-making, helping individuals to approach challenges with confidence and determination.

Known for its ability to amplify healing energies, Hematite is used to enhance both personal energy and the effectiveness of other healing crystals. It is beneficial in promoting a balanced and harmonious energy flow during healing sessions.

Hematite aids in balancing the body's subtle energies. It aligns the chakras and stabilizes emotions, fostering a harmonious internal environment that supports emotional and physical well-being.

Utilized in various forms such as raw crystals, jewelry, and meditation tools, Hematite is a key component in holistic healing practices. It is often used in energy layouts to align and balance the body's energy centers.

Physical Healing Properties

Hematite is believed to boost physical vitality and energy levels. It helps to invigorate the body, enhancing stamina and overall health.

This crystal supports healthy blood circulation and detoxification. It helps to purify the blood and strengthen the cardiovascular system, contributing to overall vitality and well-being.

Hematite aids in detoxifying the body, supporting liver function and cleansing the system of toxins. This contributes to improved metabolic health and overall well-being.

Hematite supports bone and joint health, helping to strengthen bones and alleviate joint pain. It is beneficial for those dealing with arthritis and other joint-related issues.

Hematite supports the body's natural healing processes by promoting cellular regeneration. It aids in the recovery from injuries and illnesses, speeding up the healing process.

Potential Homeopathic Uses

If Hematite were to be used as a homeopathic remedy, its indications might include:

Psychological Symptoms: Anxiety, emotional stress, and lack of focus. It may also help in cases of emotional instability and lack of clarity.

Physical Symptoms: Blood health issues, detoxification needs, and joint pain.

Behavioral Symptoms: Difficulty in coping with stress, lack of motivation, and a tendency towards emotional imbalance.

Hematite's homeopathic profile would focus on its ability to ground, protect, and invigorate, making it suitable for addressing conditions related to stress, blood health, and overall well-being.

Conclusion

Hematite is a vital crystal in holistic healing, celebrated for its grounding beauty and versatile healing properties. Whether used for stress relief, mental clarity, or as a protective talisman, Hematite serves as a potent aid in achieving physical health and spiritual harmony. Like

all alternative practices, these should be considered as complementary to conventional medical treatments.

Lodolite: Comprehensive Guide on Spiritual and Physical Healing Properties

Overview

Lodolite, also known as Garden Quartz or Shamanic Dream Quartz, is a unique crystal with inclusions that resemble miniature landscapes or gardens. This gemstone is often associated with healing and transformation. Lodolite is celebrated for its ability to enhance spiritual growth and promote overall well-being.

Spiritual and Psychic Benefits

Lodolite is renowned for its ability to alleviate stress and anxiety. Its tranquil energy promotes a sense of peace and relaxation, helping to clear the mind and reduce emotional tension. This makes it an excellent companion for meditation and spiritual practices.

Connected to the crown and third eye chakras, Lodolite enhances spiritual growth and inner vision. It encourages deep introspection and clarity, helping individuals to connect with their higher self and the spiritual realm.

Lodolite is a stone of transformation and healing. It supports the release of old patterns and facilitates the acceptance of new perspectives, aiding in profound personal and spiritual changes.

Known for its ability to amplify healing energies, Lodolite is used to enhance both personal energy and the effectiveness of other healing crystals. It is beneficial in promoting a balanced and harmonious energy flow during healing sessions.

Lodolite aids in balancing the body's subtle energies. It aligns the chakras and stabilizes emotions, fostering a harmonious internal environment that supports emotional and spiritual well-being.

Utilized in various forms such as raw crystals, jewelry, and meditation tools, Lodolite is a key component in holistic healing practices. It is often used in energy layouts to align and balance the body's energy centers.

Physical Healing Properties

Lodolite is believed to boost physical vitality and energy levels. It helps to invigorate the body, enhancing stamina and overall health.

Lodolite aids in detoxifying the body, supporting liver function and cleansing the system of toxins. This contributes to improved metabolic health and overall well-being.

Lodolite is believed to enhance the immune system, helping the body to fight off illnesses more effectively. It supports the body's natural defenses and promotes overall health and vitality.

Lodolite supports the body's natural healing processes by promoting cellular regeneration. It aids in the recovery from injuries and illnesses, speeding up the healing process.

Lodolite supports skin health by promoting cellular regeneration and healing. It aids in the treatment of skin conditions and improves the overall appearance of the skin.

Potential Homeopathic Uses

If Lodolite were to be used as a homeopathic remedy, its indications might include:

Psychological Symptoms: Anxiety, emotional stress, and lack of clarity. It may also help in cases of emotional instability and spiritual confusion.

Physical Symptoms: Detoxification needs, immune system deficiencies, and skin conditions.

Behavioral Symptoms: Difficulty in coping with stress, lack of motivation, and a tendency towards emotional imbalance.

Lodolite's homeopathic profile would focus on its ability to transform, protect, and rejuvenate, making it suitable for addressing conditions related to stress, detoxification, and overall well-being.

Conclusion

Lodolite is a vital crystal in holistic healing, celebrated for its unique beauty and versatile healing properties. Whether used for stress relief, spiritual growth, or as a transformative talisman, Lodolite serves as a potent aid in achieving physical health and spiritual harmony. Like all alternative practices, these should be considered as complementary to conventional medical treatments.

Psilomelane: Comprehensive Guide on Spiritual and Physical Healing Properties

Overview

Psilomelane, known for its striking black and silver banded appearance, is a powerful crystal valued for its grounding and protective energy. This gemstone is often associated with emotional healing and clarity. Psilomelane is celebrated for its ability to enhance mental focus and promote overall well-being.

Spiritual and Psychic Benefits

Psilomelane is renowned for its ability to alleviate stress and anxiety. Its grounding energy promotes a sense of stability and calm, helping to clear the mind and reduce emotional tension. This makes it an excellent companion for meditation and stress management practices.

Connected to the root and sacral chakras, Psilomelane enhances emotional healing and resilience. It encourages the release of negative emotions and supports emotional balance, helping individuals to achieve a harmonious state of mind.

Psilomelane is a stone of mental clarity and focus. It supports clear thinking and decision-making, helping individuals to approach challenges with confidence and determination.

Known for its ability to amplify healing energies, Psilomelane is used to enhance both personal energy and the effectiveness of other healing crystals. It is beneficial in promoting a balanced and harmonious energy flow during healing sessions.

Psilomelane aids in balancing the body's subtle energies. It aligns the chakras and stabilizes emotions, fostering a harmonious internal environment that supports emotional and physical well-being.

Utilized in various forms such as raw crystals, jewelry, and meditation tools, Psilomelane is a key component in holistic healing practices. It is often used in energy layouts to align and balance the body's energy centers.

Physical Healing Properties

Psilomelane is believed to boost physical vitality and energy levels. It helps to invigorate the body, enhancing stamina and overall health.

Psilomelane is believed to enhance the immune system, helping the body to fight off illnesses more effectively. It supports the body's natural defenses and promotes overall health and vitality.

Psilomelane aids in detoxifying the body, supporting liver function and cleansing the system of toxins. This contributes to improved metabolic health and overall well-being.

Psilomelane supports bone and joint health, helping to strengthen bones and alleviate joint pain. It is beneficial for those dealing with arthritis and other joint-related issues.

Psilomelane supports the body's natural healing processes by promoting cellular regeneration. It aids in the recovery from injuries and illnesses, speeding up the healing process.

Potential Homeopathic Uses

If Psilomelane were to be used as a homeopathic remedy, its indications might include:

Psychological Symptoms: Anxiety, emotional stress, and lack of clarity. It may also help in cases of emotional instability and difficulty focusing.

Physical Symptoms: Immune system deficiencies, detoxification needs, and joint pain.

Behavioral Symptoms: Difficulty in coping with stress, lack of motivation, and a tendency towards emotional imbalance.

Psilomelane's homeopathic profile would focus on its ability to ground, protect, and clarify, making it suitable for addressing conditions related to stress, immune health, and overall well-being.

Conclusion

Psilomelane is a vital crystal in holistic healing, celebrated for its grounding beauty and versatile healing properties. Whether used for stress relief, emotional healing, or as a protective talisman, Psilomelane serves as a potent aid in achieving physical health and spiritual harmony. Like all alternative practices, these should be considered as complementary to conventional medical treatments.

Realgar: Comprehensive Guide on Spiritual and Physical Healing Properties

Overview

Realgar, known for its vivid red to orange color, is a rare and powerful crystal valued for its transformative and energizing properties. This gemstone is often associated with passion and vitality. Realgar is celebrated for its ability to enhance creativity and promote overall well-being.

Spiritual and Psychic Benefits

Realgar is renowned for its ability to alleviate stress and anxiety. Its vibrant energy promotes a sense of joy and enthusiasm, helping to uplift the spirit and dispel negative emotions. This makes it an excellent companion for meditation and stress management practices.

Connected to the sacral chakra, Realgar enhances creativity and passion. It encourages self-expression and inspires new ideas, making it a powerful tool for artists and creators.

Realgar is a stone of transformation and growth. It supports the release of old patterns and the acceptance of new perspectives, facilitating profound changes in one's personal and spiritual journey.

Known for its ability to amplify healing energies, Realgar is used to enhance both personal energy and the effectiveness of other healing crystals. It is beneficial in promoting a balanced and harmonious energy flow during healing sessions.

Realgar aids in balancing the body's subtle energies. It aligns the chakras and stabilizes emotions, fostering a harmonious internal environment that supports emotional and physical well-being.

Utilized in various forms such as raw crystals, jewelry, and meditation tools, Realgar is a key component in holistic healing practices. It is often used in energy layouts to align and balance the body's energy centers.

Physical Healing Properties

Realgar is believed to boost physical vitality and energy levels. It helps to invigorate the body, enhancing stamina and overall health.

Realgar aids in detoxifying the body, supporting liver function and cleansing the system of toxins. This contributes to improved metabolic health and overall well-being.

Realgar is believed to enhance the immune system, helping the body to fight off illnesses more effectively. It supports the body's natural defenses and promotes overall health and vitality.

Realgar supports reproductive health, helping to balance hormonal levels and enhance fertility. It is beneficial for those dealing with reproductive issues.

Realgar supports the body's natural healing processes by promoting cellular regeneration. It aids in the recovery from injuries and illnesses, speeding up the healing process.

Potential Homeopathic Uses

If Realgar were to be used as a homeopathic remedy, its indications might include:

Psychological Symptoms: Anxiety, low self-esteem, and lack of motivation. It may also help in cases of emotional instability and lack of passion.

Physical Symptoms: Reproductive health issues, detoxification needs, and immune system deficiencies.

Behavioral Symptoms: Difficulty in coping with stress, lack of creativity, and a tendency towards emotional imbalance.

Realgar's homeopathic profile would focus on its ability to invigorate, transform, and inspire, making it suitable for addressing conditions related to stress, reproductive health, and overall well-being.

Conclusion

Realgar is a vital crystal in holistic healing, celebrated for its vibrant beauty and versatile healing properties. Whether used for stress relief, personal empowerment, or as a transformative talisman, Realgar serves as a potent aid in achieving physical health and spiritual harmony. Like

all alternative practices, these should be considered as complementary to conventional medical treatments.

Wavellite: Comprehensive Guide on Spiritual and Physical Healing Properties

Overview

Wavellite, known for its beautiful radial clusters of green to yellow-green hues, is a unique crystal appreciated for its soothing and harmonizing energy. This gemstone is often associated with balance and insight. Wavellite is celebrated for its ability to enhance mental clarity and promote overall well-being.

Spiritual and Psychic Benefits

Wavellite is renowned for its ability to alleviate stress and anxiety. Its calming energy promotes a sense of peace and relaxation, helping to clear the mind and reduce emotional tension. This makes it an excellent companion for meditation and stress management practices.

Connected to the heart and third eye chakras, Wavellite enhances mental clarity and insight. It encourages clear thinking and decision-making, helping individuals to approach challenges with confidence and understanding.

Wavellite is a stone of emotional balance and harmony. It supports the release of negative emotions and promotes emotional healing, helping individuals to achieve a harmonious state of mind.

Known for its ability to amplify healing energies, Wavellite is used to enhance both personal energy and the effectiveness of other healing crystals. It is beneficial in promoting a balanced and harmonious energy flow during healing sessions.

Wavellite aids in balancing the body's subtle energies. It aligns the chakras and stabilizes emotions, fostering a harmonious internal environment that supports emotional and spiritual well-being.

Utilized in various forms such as raw crystals, jewelry, and meditation tools, Wavellite is a key component in holistic healing practices. It is often used in energy layouts to align and balance the body's energy centers.

Physical Healing Properties

Wavellite is believed to boost physical vitality and energy levels. It helps to invigorate the body, enhancing stamina and overall health.

Wavellite is believed to enhance the immune system, helping the body to fight off illnesses more effectively. It supports the body's natural defenses and promotes overall health and vitality.

Wavellite aids in detoxifying the body, supporting liver function and cleansing the system of toxins. This contributes to improved metabolic health and overall well-being.

Wavellite supports the body's natural healing processes by promoting cellular regeneration. It aids in the recovery from injuries and illnesses, speeding up the healing process.

Wavellite supports digestive health by promoting a healthy digestive system. It helps to alleviate issues such as indigestion and stomach discomfort, contributing to overall digestive well-being.

Potential Homeopathic Uses

If Wavellite were to be used as a homeopathic remedy, its indications might include:

Psychological Symptoms: Anxiety, emotional stress, and lack of clarity. It may also help in cases of emotional instability and difficulty focusing.

Physical Symptoms: Immune system deficiencies, detoxification needs, and digestive issues.

Behavioral Symptoms: Difficulty in coping with stress, lack of motivation, and a tendency towards emotional imbalance.

Wavellite's homeopathic profile would focus on its ability to clarify, protect, and harmonize, making it suitable for addressing conditions related to stress, immune health, and overall well-being.

Conclusion

Wavellite is a vital crystal in holistic healing, celebrated for its soothing beauty and versatile healing properties. Whether used for stress relief, mental clarity, or as a harmonizing talisman, Wavellite serves as a potent aid in achieving physical health and spiritual harmony. Like all alternative practices, these should be considered as complementary to conventional medical treatments.

Bytownite: Comprehensive Guide on Spiritual and Physical Healing Properties

Overview

Bytownite, known for its translucent to opaque appearance with colors ranging from yellow to greenish-yellow, is a captivating crystal appreciated for its grounding and stabilizing energy. This gemstone is often associated with strength and clarity. Bytownite is celebrated for its ability to enhance mental focus and promote overall well-being.

Spiritual and Psychic Benefits

Bytownite is renowned for its ability to alleviate stress and anxiety. Its grounding energy promotes a sense of stability and calm, helping to clear the mind and reduce emotional tension. This makes it an excellent companion for meditation and stress management practices.

Connected to the solar plexus and root chakras, Bytownite enhances mental clarity and focus. It encourages clear thinking and decision-making, helping individuals to approach challenges with confidence and understanding.

Bytownite is a stone of emotional strength and resilience. It supports the release of negative emotions and promotes emotional balance, helping individuals to achieve a harmonious state of mind.

Known for its ability to amplify healing energies, Bytownite is used to enhance both personal energy and the effectiveness of other healing crystals. It is beneficial in promoting a balanced and harmonious energy flow during healing sessions.

Bytownite aids in balancing the body's subtle energies. It aligns the chakras and stabilizes emotions, fostering a harmonious internal environment that supports emotional and physical well-being.

Utilized in various forms such as raw crystals, jewelry, and meditation tools, Bytownite is a key component in holistic healing practices. It is often used in energy layouts to align and balance the body's energy centers.

Physical Healing Properties

Bytownite is believed to boost physical vitality and energy levels. It helps to invigorate the body, enhancing stamina and overall health.

Bytownite supports digestive health by promoting a healthy digestive system. It helps to alleviate issues such as indigestion and stomach discomfort, contributing to overall digestive well-being.

Bytownite aids in detoxifying the body, supporting liver function and cleansing the system of toxins. This contributes to improved metabolic health and overall well-being.

Bytownite is believed to enhance the immune system, helping the body to fight off illnesses more effectively. It supports the body's natural defenses and promotes overall health and vitality.

Bytownite supports bone and joint health, helping to strengthen bones and alleviate joint pain. It is beneficial for those dealing with arthritis and other joint-related issues.

Potential Homeopathic Uses

If Bytownite were to be used as a homeopathic remedy, its indications might include:

Psychological Symptoms: Anxiety, emotional stress, and lack of clarity. It may also help in cases of emotional instability and difficulty focusing.

Physical Symptoms: Digestive health issues, detoxification needs, and immune system deficiencies.

Behavioral Symptoms: Difficulty in coping with stress, lack of motivation, and a tendency towards emotional imbalance.

Bytownite's homeopathic profile would focus on its ability to ground, protect, and clarify, making it suitable for addressing conditions related to stress, digestive health, and overall well-being.

Conclusion

Bytownite is a vital crystal in holistic healing, celebrated for its grounding beauty and versatile healing properties. Whether used for stress relief, mental clarity, or as a protective talisman, Bytownite serves as a potent aid in achieving physical health and spiritual harmony. Like

all alternative practices, these should be considered as complementary to conventional medical treatments.

Tantalite: Comprehensive Guide on Spiritual and Physical Healing Properties

Overview

Tantalite, known for its dark to black metallic appearance, is a powerful and grounding crystal valued for its protective and stabilizing energy. This gemstone is often associated with strength and resilience. Tantalite is celebrated for its ability to enhance focus and promote overall well-being.

Spiritual and Psychic Benefits

Tantalite is renowned for its ability to alleviate stress and anxiety. Its grounding energy promotes a sense of stability and calm, helping to clear the mind and reduce emotional tension. This makes it an excellent companion for meditation and stress management practices.

Connected to the root chakra, Tantalite enhances grounding and protection. It encourages a strong connection to the earth, helping individuals to feel secure and centered.

Tantalite is a stone of mental clarity and focus. It supports clear thinking and decision-making, helping individuals to approach challenges with confidence and determination.

Known for its ability to amplify healing energies, Tantalite is used to enhance both personal energy and the effectiveness of other healing crystals. It is beneficial in promoting a balanced and harmonious energy flow during healing sessions.

Tantalite aids in balancing the body's subtle energies. It aligns the chakras and stabilizes emotions, fostering a harmonious internal environment that supports emotional and physical well-being.

Utilized in various forms such as raw crystals, jewelry, and meditation tools, Tantalite is a key component in holistic healing practices. It is often used in energy layouts to align and balance the body's energy centers.

Physical Healing Properties

Tantalite is believed to boost physical vitality and energy levels. It helps to invigorate the body, enhancing stamina and overall health.

Tantalite supports bone and joint health, helping to strengthen bones and alleviate joint pain. It is beneficial for those dealing with arthritis and other joint-related issues.

Tantalite aids in detoxifying the body, supporting liver function and cleansing the system of toxins. This contributes to improved metabolic health and overall well-being.

Tantalite is believed to enhance the immune system, helping the body to fight off illnesses more effectively. It supports the body's natural defenses and promotes overall health and vitality.

Tantalite supports the body's natural healing processes by promoting cellular regeneration. It aids in the recovery from injuries and illnesses, speeding up the healing process.

Potential Homeopathic Uses

If Tantalite were to be used as a homeopathic remedy, its indications might include:

Psychological Symptoms: Anxiety, emotional stress, and lack of clarity. It may also help in cases of emotional instability and difficulty focusing.

Physical Symptoms: Bone and joint health issues, detoxification needs, and immune system deficiencies.

Behavioral Symptoms: Difficulty in coping with stress, lack of motivation, and a tendency towards emotional imbalance.

Tantalite's homeopathic profile would focus on its ability to ground, protect, and clarify, making it suitable for addressing conditions related to stress, bone health, and overall well-being.

Conclusion

Tantalite is a vital crystal in holistic healing, celebrated for its grounding beauty and versatile healing properties. Whether used for stress relief, mental clarity, or as a protective talisman, Tantalite serves as a potent aid in achieving physical health and spiritual harmony. Like

all alternative practices, these should be considered as complementary to conventional medical treatments.

Heliodor: Comprehensive Guide on Spiritual and Physical Healing Properties

Overview

Heliodor, known for its brilliant yellow to golden hues, is a vibrant crystal valued for its energizing and uplifting energy. This gemstone is often associated with clarity and personal power. Heliodor is celebrated for its ability to enhance confidence and promote overall well-being

.

Spiritual and Psychic Benefits

Heliodor is renowned for its ability to alleviate stress and anxiety. Its uplifting energy promotes a sense of joy and optimism, helping to clear the mind and reduce emotional tension. This makes it an excellent companion for meditation and stress management practices.

Connected to the solar plexus chakra, Heliodor enhances personal power and confidence. It encourages self-expression and assertiveness, helping individuals to pursue their goals with determination and enthusiasm.

Heliodor is a stone of clarity and insight. It supports clear thinking and decision-making, helping individuals to approach challenges with confidence and understanding.

Known for its ability to amplify healing energies, Heliodor is used to enhance both personal energy and the effectiveness of other healing crystals. It is beneficial in promoting a balanced and harmonious energy flow during healing sessions.

Heliodor aids in balancing the body's subtle energies. It aligns the chakras and stabilizes emotions, fostering a harmonious internal environment that supports emotional and mental well-being.

Utilized in various forms such as raw crystals, jewelry, and meditation tools, Heliodor is a key component in holistic healing practices. It is often used in energy layouts to align and balance the body's energy centers.

Physical Healing Properties

Heliodor is believed to boost physical vitality and energy levels. It helps to invigorate the body, enhancing stamina and overall health.

Heliodor supports digestive health by promoting a healthy digestive system. It helps to alleviate issues such as indigestion and stomach discomfort, contributing to overall digestive well-being.

Heliodor is believed to enhance the immune system, helping the body to fight off illnesses more effectively. It supports the body's natural defenses and promotes overall health and vitality.

Heliodor aids in detoxifying the body, supporting liver function and cleansing the system of toxins. This contributes to improved metabolic health and overall well-being.

Heliodor supports the body's natural healing processes by promoting cellular regeneration. It aids in the recovery from injuries and illnesses, speeding up the healing process.

Potential Homeopathic Uses

If Heliodor were to be used as a homeopathic remedy, its indications might include:

Psychological Symptoms: Anxiety, low self-esteem, and lack of motivation. It may also help in cases of emotional instability and lack of clarity.

Physical Symptoms: Digestive health issues, immune system deficiencies, and detoxification needs.

Behavioral Symptoms: Difficulty in coping with stress, lack of confidence, and a tendency towards emotional imbalance.

Heliodor's homeopathic profile would focus on its ability to invigorate, protect, and clarify, making it suitable for addressing conditions related to stress, digestive health, and overall well-being.

Conclusion

Heliodor is a vital crystal in holistic healing, celebrated for its vibrant beauty and versatile healing properties. Whether used for stress relief, personal empowerment, or as a clarifying talisman, Heliodor serves as a potent aid in achieving physical health and spiritual

harmony. Like all alternative practices, these should be considered as complementary to conventional medical treatments.

Larvikite: Comprehensive Guide on Spiritual and Physical Healing Properties

Overview

Larvikite, known for its striking blue and silver flashes, is a captivating crystal appreciated for its protective and grounding energy. This gemstone is often associated with earth connection and psychic abilities. Larvikite is celebrated for its ability to enhance intuition and promote overall well-being.

Spiritual and Psychic Benefits

Larvikite is renowned for its ability to alleviate stress and anxiety. Its grounding energy promotes a sense of peace and stability, helping to calm the mind and body. This makes it an excellent companion for meditation and relaxation practices.

Connected to the third eye and root chakras, Larvikite enhances intuition and psychic abilities. It encourages clear thinking and spiritual insight, helping individuals to connect with their inner guidance and the natural world.

Larvikite acts as a protective shield against negative energies and psychic attacks. It is particularly effective in safeguarding against emotional and spiritual harm, creating a safe and nurturing environment for spiritual activities.

Known for its ability to amplify healing energies, Larvikite is used to enhance both personal energy and the effectiveness of other healing crystals. It is beneficial in promoting a balanced and harmonious energy flow during healing sessions.

Larvikite aids in balancing the body's subtle energies. It aligns the chakras and stabilizes emotions, fostering a harmonious internal environment that supports emotional and spiritual well-being.

Utilized in various forms such as raw crystals, jewelry, and meditation tools, Larvikite is a key component in holistic healing practices. It is often used in energy layouts to align and balance the body's energy centers.

Physical Healing Properties

Larvikite is believed to boost physical vitality and energy levels. It helps to invigorate the body, enhancing stamina and overall health.

Larvikite aids in detoxifying the body, supporting liver function and cleansing the system of toxins. This contributes to improved metabolic health and overall well-being.

Larvikite is associated with enhancing cognitive function. It supports mental clarity, focus, and decision-making, making it beneficial for those dealing with mental fatigue and confusion.

Larvikite is believed to enhance the immune system, helping the body to fight off illnesses more effectively. It supports the body's natural defenses and promotes overall health and vitality.

Larvikite supports skin health by promoting cellular regeneration. It aids in the healing of skin conditions and improves the overall appearance of the skin.

Potential Homeopathic Uses

If Larvikite were to be used as a homeopathic remedy, its indications might include:

Psychological Symptoms: Anxiety, mental fatigue, and stress. It may also help in cases of emotional instability and lack of focus.

Physical Symptoms: Detoxification needs, immune system support, and skin conditions.

Behavioral Symptoms: Difficulty in coping with stress, lack of motivation, and a tendency towards emotional imbalance.

Larvikite's homeopathic profile would focus on its ability to ground, protect, and invigorate, making it suitable for addressing conditions related to stress, cognitive function, and overall well-being.

Conclusion

Larvikite is a vital crystal in holistic healing, celebrated for its grounding beauty and versatile healing properties. Whether used for stress relief, intuitive enhancement, or as a protective talisman, Larvikite serves as a potent aid in achieving physical health and spiritual harmony. Like all alternative practices, these should be considered as complementary to conventional medical treatments.

Chrysoberyl: Comprehensive Guide on Spiritual and Physical Healing Properties

Overview

Chrysoberyl, known for its vibrant yellow-green color and cat's eye effect, is a remarkable crystal valued for its clarity and protective energy. This gemstone is often associated with personal power and insight. Chrysoberyl is celebrated for its ability to enhance self-confidence and promote overall well-being.

Spiritual and Psychic Benefits

Chrysoberyl is renowned for its ability to alleviate stress and anxiety. Its clear and focused energy promotes a sense of peace and clarity, helping to calm the mind and body. This makes it an excellent companion for meditation and stress management practices.

Connected to the solar plexus chakra, Chrysoberyl enhances self-confidence and personal power. It encourages clarity of thought and decision-making, helping individuals to approach challenges with confidence and determination.

Chrysoberyl acts as a protective shield against negative energies and psychic attacks. It is particularly effective in safeguarding against emotional and spiritual harm, creating a safe and nurturing environment for spiritual activities.

Known for its ability to amplify healing energies, Chrysoberyl is used to enhance both personal energy and the effectiveness of other healing crystals. It is beneficial in promoting a balanced and harmonious energy flow during healing sessions.

Chrysoberyl aids in balancing the body's subtle energies. It aligns the chakras and stabilizes emotions, fostering a harmonious internal environment that supports emotional and spiritual well-being.

Utilized in various forms such as raw crystals, jewelry, and meditation tools, Chrysoberyl is a key component in holistic healing practices. It is often used in energy layouts to align and balance the body's energy centers.

Physical Healing Properties

Chrysoberyl is believed to boost physical vitality and energy levels. It helps to invigorate the body, enhancing stamina and overall health.

This crystal is traditionally associated with eye health. It is believed to strengthen vision and protect against eye-related issues, enhancing clarity and focus.

Chrysoberyl aids in detoxifying the body, supporting liver function and cleansing the system of toxins. This contributes to improved metabolic health and overall well-being.

Chrysoberyl supports bone and muscle health, helping to strengthen bones and alleviate muscle pain. It is beneficial for those dealing with physical strain and injuries.

Chrysoberyl supports the body's natural healing processes by promoting cellular regeneration. It aids in the recovery from injuries and illnesses, speeding up the healing process.

Potential Homeopathic Uses

If Chrysoberyl were to be used as a homeopathic remedy, its indications might include:

Psychological Symptoms: Anxiety, lack of confidence, and mental fatigue. It may also help in cases of emotional instability and indecision.

Physical Symptoms: Eye health issues, detoxification needs, and muscle pain.

Behavioral Symptoms: Difficulty in coping with stress, lack of motivation, and a tendency towards emotional imbalance.

Chrysoberyl's homeopathic profile would focus on its ability to clarify, protect, and invigorate, making it suitable for addressing conditions related to stress, eye health, and overall well-being.

Conclusion

Chrysoberyl is a vital crystal in holistic healing, celebrated for its vibrant beauty and versatile healing properties. Whether used for stress relief, personal empowerment, or as a protective talisman, Chrysoberyl serves as a potent aid in achieving physical health and spiritual

harmony. Like all alternative practices, these should be considered as complementary to conventional medical treatments.

Idocrase: Comprehensive Guide on Spiritual and Physical Healing Properties

Overview

Idocrase, also known as Vesuvianite, is a captivating crystal with colors ranging from green to brown. This gemstone is often associated with personal growth and transformation. Idocrase is celebrated for its ability to enhance mental clarity and promote overall well-being.

Spiritual and Psychic Benefits

Idocrase is renowned for its ability to alleviate stress and anxiety. Its soothing energy promotes a sense of peace and tranquility, helping to calm the mind and body. This makes it an excellent companion for meditation and stress management practices.

Connected to the heart and solar plexus chakras, Idocrase enhances personal growth and self-discovery. It encourages confidence and clarity, helping individuals to explore their true potential and purpose.

Idocrase is a stone of transformation, aiding in the release of old patterns and the acceptance of new beginnings. It supports spiritual evolution and helps individuals navigate life changes with grace and resilience.

Known for its ability to amplify healing energies, Idocrase is used to enhance both personal energy and the effectiveness of other healing crystals. It is beneficial in promoting a balanced and harmonious energy flow during healing sessions.

Idocrase aids in balancing the body's subtle energies. It aligns the chakras and stabilizes emotions, fostering a harmonious internal environment that supports emotional and spiritual well-being.

Utilized in various forms such as raw crystals, jewelry, and meditation tools, Idocrase is a key component in holistic healing practices. It is often used in energy layouts to align and balance the body's energy centers.

Physical Healing Properties

Idocrase is believed to boost physical vitality and energy levels. It helps to invigorate the body, enhancing stamina and overall health.

This crystal supports the digestive system, helping to alleviate issues such as indigestion and stomach discomfort. It promotes a healthy digestive process and aids in nutrient absorption.

Idocrase aids in detoxifying the body, supporting liver function and cleansing the system of toxins. This contributes to improved metabolic health and overall well-being.

Idocrase supports the body's natural healing processes by promoting cellular regeneration. It aids in the recovery from injuries and illnesses, speeding up the healing process.

Idocrase is believed to support bone and joint health, helping to strengthen bones and alleviate joint pain. It is beneficial for those dealing with arthritis and other joint-related issues.

Potential Homeopathic Uses

If Idocrase were to be used as a homeopathic remedy, its indications might include:

Psychological Symptoms: Anxiety, emotional stress, and lack of clarity. It may also help in cases of emotional instability and indecision.

Physical Symptoms: Digestive health issues, detoxification needs, and joint pain.

Behavioral Symptoms: Difficulty in coping with stress, lack of motivation, and a tendency towards emotional imbalance.

Idocrase's homeopathic profile would focus on its ability to transform, clarify, and invigorate, making it suitable for addressing conditions related to stress, digestive health, and overall well-being.

Conclusion

Idocrase is a vital crystal in holistic healing, celebrated for its transformative beauty and versatile healing properties. Whether used for stress relief, personal growth, or as a talisman for transformation, Idocrase serves as a potent aid in achieving physical health and spiritual

harmony. Like all alternative practices, these should be considered as complementary to conventional medical treatments.

Mookaite: Comprehensive Guide on Spiritual and Physical Healing Properties

Overview

Mookaite, also known as Mookaite Jasper, is a vibrant crystal with colors ranging from red and yellow to purple and brown. This gemstone is often associated with grounding and vitality. Mookaite is celebrated for its ability to enhance personal strength and promote overall well-being.

Spiritual and Psychic Benefits

Mookaite is renowned for its ability to alleviate stress and anxiety. Its grounding energy promotes a sense of stability and balance, helping to calm the mind and body. This makes it an excellent companion for meditation and stress management practices.

Connected to the root chakra, Mookaite enhances grounding and stability. It encourages a strong connection to the earth, helping individuals to feel secure and centered.

Mookaite is a stone of personal strength and vitality. It supports self-confidence and courage, helping individuals to face challenges with determination and resilience.

Known for its ability to amplify healing energies, Mookaite is used to enhance both personal energy and the effectiveness of other healing crystals. It is beneficial in promoting a balanced and harmonious energy flow during healing sessions.

Mookaite aids in balancing the body's subtle energies. It aligns the chakras and stabilizes emotions, fostering a harmonious internal environment that supports emotional and physical well-being.

Utilized in various forms such as raw crystals, jewelry, and meditation tools, Mookaite is a key component in holistic healing practices. It is often used in energy layouts to align and balance the body's energy centers.

Physical Healing Properties

Mookaite is believed to boost physical vitality and energy levels. It helps to invigorate the body, enhancing stamina and overall health.

Mookaite is believed to enhance the immune system, helping the body to fight off illnesses more effectively. It supports the body's natural defenses and promotes overall health and vitality.

This crystal supports the digestive system, helping to alleviate issues such as indigestion and stomach discomfort. It promotes a healthy digestive process and aids in nutrient absorption.

Mookaite aids in detoxifying the body, supporting liver function and cleansing the system of toxins. This contributes to improved metabolic health and overall well-being.

Mookaite supports the body's natural healing processes by promoting cellular regeneration. It aids in the recovery from injuries and illnesses, speeding up the healing process.

Potential Homeopathic Uses

If Mookaite were to be used as a homeopathic remedy, its indications might include:

Psychological Symptoms: Anxiety, stress, and lack of confidence. It may also help in cases of emotional instability and lack of motivation.

Physical Symptoms: Digestive health issues, immune system deficiencies, and detoxification needs.

Behavioral Symptoms: Difficulty in coping with stress, lack of resilience, and a tendency towards emotional imbalance.

Mookaite's homeopathic profile would focus on its ability to ground, invigorate, and stabilize, making it suitable for addressing conditions related to stress, digestive health, and overall well-being.

Conclusion

Mookaite is a vital crystal in holistic healing, celebrated for its vibrant beauty and versatile healing properties. Whether used for stress relief, personal strength, or as a grounding talisman, Mookaite serves as a potent aid in achieving physical health and spiritual harmony. Like all alternative practices, these should be considered as complementary to conventional medical treatments.

Brookite: Comprehensive Guide on Spiritual and Physical Healing Properties

Overview

Brookite, known for its striking brown to black hues with shimmering inclusions, is a rare crystal valued for its high-frequency energy and transformative properties. This gemstone is often associated with spiritual awakening and clarity. Brookite is celebrated for its ability to elevate consciousness and promote overall well-being.

Spiritual and Psychic Benefits

Brookite is renowned for its ability to alleviate stress and anxiety. Its high-frequency energy promotes a sense of calm and tranquility, helping to clear the mind and reduce emotional tension. This makes it an excellent companion for meditation and spiritual practices.

Connected to the crown and third eye chakras, Brookite enhances spiritual awakening and higher consciousness. It encourages clarity of thought and spiritual insight, helping individuals to connect with their higher self and the universe.

Brookite is a stone of transformation, aiding in personal and spiritual growth. It supports the release of old patterns and the acceptance of new perspectives, facilitating profound changes in one's life.

Known for its ability to amplify healing energies, Brookite is used to enhance both personal energy and the effectiveness of other healing crystals. It is beneficial in promoting a balanced and harmonious energy flow during healing sessions.

Brookite aids in balancing the body's subtle energies. It aligns the chakras and stabilizes emotions, fostering a harmonious internal environment that supports spiritual and emotional well-being.

Utilized in various forms such as raw crystals, jewelry, and meditation tools, Brookite is a key component in holistic healing practices. It is often used in energy layouts to align and balance the body's energy centers.

Physical Healing Properties

Brookite is believed to boost physical vitality and energy levels. It helps to invigorate the body, enhancing stamina and overall health.

Brookite aids in detoxifying the body, supporting liver function and cleansing the system of toxins. This contributes to improved metabolic health and overall well-being.

Brookite supports the body's natural healing processes by promoting cellular regeneration. It aids in the recovery from injuries and illnesses, speeding up the healing process.

Brookite is believed to enhance the immune system, helping the body to fight off illnesses more effectively. It supports the body's natural defenses and promotes overall health and vitality.

Brookite supports bone and joint health, helping to strengthen bones and alleviate joint pain. It is beneficial for those dealing with arthritis and other joint-related issues.

Potential Homeopathic Uses

If Brookite were to be used as a homeopathic remedy, its indications might include:

Psychological Symptoms: Anxiety, mental fatigue, and lack of clarity. It may also help in cases of emotional instability and spiritual confusion.

Physical Symptoms: Detoxification needs, immune system deficiencies, and joint pain.

Behavioral Symptoms: Difficulty in coping with stress, lack of motivation, and a tendency towards emotional imbalance.

Brookite's homeopathic profile would focus on its ability to transform, clarify, and invigorate, making it suitable for addressing conditions related to stress, detoxification, and overall well-being.

Conclusion

Brookite is a vital crystal in holistic healing, celebrated for its high-frequency energy and versatile healing properties. Whether used for stress relief, spiritual awakening, or as a transformative talisman,

Brookite serves as a potent aid in achieving physical health and spiritual harmony. Like all alternative practices, these should be considered as complementary to conventional medical treatments.

Clinozoisite: Comprehensive Guide on Spiritual and Physical Healing Properties

Overview

Clinozoisite, known for its green to brownish hues and crystalline structure, is a fascinating crystal valued for its harmonizing and restorative energy. This gemstone is often associated with emotional healing and resilience. Clinozoisite is celebrated for its ability to enhance emotional stability and promote overall well-being.

Spiritual and Psychic Benefits

Stress Relief and Calming: Clinozoisite is renowned for its ability to alleviate stress and anxiety. Its soothing energy promotes a sense of peace and balance, helping to calm the mind and body. This makes it an excellent companion for meditation and stress management practices.

Emotional Healing: Connected to the heart chakra, Clinozoisite enhances emotional healing and resilience. It encourages the release of negative emotions and supports the healing of emotional wounds, helping individuals achieve emotional balance and harmony.

Personal Growth: Clinozoisite supports personal growth and self-discovery. It encourages introspection and self-awareness, helping individuals understand and overcome personal challenges.

Enhancement of Healing Energies: Known for its ability to amplify healing energies, Clinozoisite is used to enhance both personal energy and the effectiveness of other healing crystals. It is beneficial in promoting a balanced and harmonious energy flow during healing sessions.

Harmonization and Balance:

Clinozoisite aids in balancing the body's subtle energies. It aligns the chakras and stabilizes emotions, fostering a harmonious internal environment that supports emotional and physical well-being.

Versatile Use in Healing Practices: Utilized in various forms such as raw crystals, jewelry, and meditation tools, Clinozoisite is a key component in holistic healing practices. It is often used in energy layouts to align and balance the body's energy centers.

Physical Healing Properties

Vitality and Energy: Clinozoisite is believed to boost physical vitality and energy levels. It helps invigorate the body, enhancing stamina and overall health.

Bone and Joint Health: Clinozoisite supports bone and joint health, helping to strengthen bones and alleviate joint pain. It is beneficial for those dealing with arthritis and other joint-related issues.

Detoxification: Clinozoisite aids in detoxifying the body, supporting liver function and cleansing the system of toxins. This contributes to improved metabolic health and overall well-being.

Cellular Regeneration: Clinozoisite supports the body's natural healing processes by promoting cellular regeneration. It aids in the recovery from injuries and illnesses, speeding up the healing process.

Immune System: Clinozoisite is believed to enhance the immune system, helping the body fight off illnesses more effectively. It supports the body's natural defenses and promotes overall health and vitality.

.Potential Homeopathic Uses

If Clinozoisite were to be used as a homeopathic remedy, its indications might include:

Psychological Symptoms: Anxiety, emotional stress, and lack of clarity. It may also help in cases of emotional instability and vulnerability.

Physical Symptoms: Bone and joint health issues, detoxification needs, and energy depletion.

Behavioral Symptoms : Difficulty in coping with stress, lack of motivation, and a tendency towards emotional imbalance.

Clinozoisite's homeopathic profile would focus on its ability to heal, protect, and stabilize, making it suitable for addressing conditions related to stress, bone health, and overall well-being.

Conclusion

Clinozoisite is a vital crystal in holistic healing, celebrated for its harmonizing beauty and versatile healing properties. Whether used for stress relief, emotional healing, or as a restorative talisman, Clinozoisite serves as a potent aid in achieving physical health and spiritual harmony. Like all alternative practices, these should be considered as complementary to conventional medical treatments.

Covellite: Comprehensive Guide on Spiritual and Physical Healing Properties

Overview

Covellite, known for its deep blue and metallic sheen, is a captivating crystal cherished for its transformative and metaphysical properties. This gemstone is often associated with deep insight and spiritual evolution. Covellite is celebrated for its ability to enhance psychic abilities and promote overall well-being.

Spiritual and Psychic Benefits

Stress Relief and Calming: Covellite is renowned for its ability to alleviate stress and anxiety. Its calming energy promotes a sense of peace and tranquility, helping to clear the mind and reduce emotional tension. This makes it an excellent companion for meditation and spiritual practices.

Psychic Abilities: Connected to the third eye and crown chakras, Covellite enhances psychic abilities and intuition. It encourages deep insight and spiritual clarity, helping individuals connect with their higher self and the metaphysical realm.

Spiritual Evolution: Covellite is a stone of transformation and spiritual evolution. It aids in the release of old patterns and the acceptance of new perspectives, facilitating profound changes in one's spiritual journey.

Enhancement of Healing Energies: Known for its ability to amplify healing energies, Covellite is used to enhance both personal energy and the effectiveness of other healing crystals. It is beneficial in promoting a balanced and harmonious energy flow during healing sessions.

Harmonization and Balance: Covellite aids in balancing the body's subtle energies. It aligns the chakras and stabilizes emotions, fostering a harmonious internal environment that supports spiritual and emotional well-being.

Versatile Use in Healing Practices: Utilized in various forms such as raw crystals, jewelry, and meditation tools, Covellite is a key component in holistic healing practices. It is often used in energy layouts to align and balance the body's energy centers.

Physical Healing Properties

Vitality and Energy: Covellite is believed to boost physical vitality and energy levels. It helps invigorate the body, enhancing stamina and overall health.

Detoxification: Covellite aids in detoxifying the body, supporting liver function and cleansing the system of toxins. This contributes to improved metabolic health and overall well-being.

Cellular Regeneration:Covellite supports the body's natural healing processes by promoting cellular regeneration. It aids in the recovery from injuries and illnesses, speeding up the healing process.

Immune System: Covellite is believed to enhance the immune system, helping the body to fight off illnesses more effectively. It supports the body's natural defenses and promotes overall health and vitality.

Skin Health: Covellite supports skin health by promoting cellular regeneration and healing. It aids in the treatment of skin conditions and improves the overall appearance of the skin.

Potential Homeopathic Uses

If Covellite were to be used as a homeopathic remedy, its indications might include:

Psychological Symptoms: Anxiety, emotional stress, and lack of clarity. It may also help in cases of emotional instability and spiritual confusion.

Physical Symptoms: Detoxification needs, immune system deficiencies, and skin conditions.

Behavioral Symptoms: Difficulty in coping with stress, lack of motivation, and a tendency towards emotional imbalance.

Covellite's homeopathic profile would focus on its ability to transform, clarify, and rejuvenate, making it suitable for addressing conditions related to stress, detoxification, and overall well-being.

Conclusion

Covellite is a vital crystal in holistic healing, celebrated for its deep beauty and versatile healing properties. Whether used for stress relief, psychic enhancement, or as a transformative talisman, Covellite serves as a potent aid in achieving physical health and spiritual harmony. Like all alternative practices, these should be considered as complementary to conventional medical treatments.

Eilat Stone: Comprehensive Guide on Spiritual and Physical Healing Properties

Overview

Eilat Stone, known for its vibrant mix of blue, green, and turquoise colors, is a unique crystal valued for its rich mineral composition and healing energy. This gemstone is often associated with balance and harmony. Eilat Stone is celebrated for its ability to enhance emotional and physical well-being.

Spiritual and Psychic Benefits

Stress Relief and Calming: Eilat Stone is renowned for its ability to alleviate stress and anxiety. Its soothing energy promotes a sense of peace and relaxation, helping to calm the mind and body. This makes it an excellent companion for meditation and stress management practices.

Emotional Balance: Connected to the heart and throat chakras, Eilat Stone enhances emotional balance and communication. It encourages emotional healing and helps individuals express their feelings more effectively.

Harmony and Integration: Eilat Stone is a stone of balance and integration. It aids in harmonizing different aspects of oneself, promoting a sense of unity and wholeness. This supports personal growth and self-acceptance.

Enhancement of Healing Energies: Known for its ability to amplify healing energies, Eilat Stone is used to enhance both personal energy and the effectiveness of other healing crystals. It is beneficial in promoting a balanced and harmonious energy flow during healing sessions.

Harmonization and Balance: Eilat Stone aids in balancing the body's subtle energies. It aligns the chakras and stabilizes emotions, fostering a harmonious internal environment that supports emotional and physical well-being.

Versatile Use in Healing Practices: Utilized in various forms such as raw crystals, jewelry, and meditation tools, Eilat Stone is a key component in holistic healing practices. It is often used in energy layouts to align and balance the body's energy centers.

Physical Healing Properties

Vitality and Energy: Eilat Stone is believed to boost physical vitality and energy levels. It helps invigorate the body, enhancing stamina and overall health.

Immune System:Eilat Stone is believed to enhance the immune system, helping the body to fight off illnesses more effectively. It supports the body's natural defenses and promotes overall health and vitality.

Pain Relief: This crystal supports pain relief, especially for joint and muscle pain. It helps alleviate discomfort and promote overall well-being.

Detoxification: Eilat Stone aids in detoxifying the body, supporting liver function and cleansing the system of toxins. This contributes to improved metabolic health and overall well-being.

Healing and Regeneration: Eilat Stone supports the body's natural healing processes by promoting cellular regeneration. It aids in the recovery from injuries and illnesses, speeding up the healing process.

Potential Homeopathic Uses

If this were to be used as a homeopathic remedy, its indications might include:

Psychological Symptoms: Anxiety, emotional stress, and lack of clarity. It may also help in cases of emotional instability and difficulty in communication.

Physical Symptoms: Immune system deficiencies, detoxification needs, and joint pain.

Behavioral Symptoms: Difficulty in coping with stress, lack of motivation, and a tendency towards emotional imbalance.

Eilat Stone's homeopathic profile would focus on its ability to balance, protect, and rejuvenate, making it suitable for addressing conditions related to stress, immune health, and overall well-being.

Conclusion

Eilat Stone is a vital crystal in holistic healing, celebrated for its vibrant beauty and versatile healing properties. Whether used for stress relief, emotional balance, or as a harmonizing talisman, Eilat Stone serves as a potent aid in achieving physical health and spiritual harmony. Like all alternative practices, these should be considered as complementary to conventional medical treatments.

Galaxite: Comprehensive Guide on Spiritual and Physical Healing Properties

Overview

Galaxite, known for its shimmering, dark blue-black appearance with flashes of iridescent colors, is a mystical crystal valued for its cosmic energy and transformative properties. This gemstone is often associated with spiritual growth and protection. Galaxite is celebrated for its ability to enhance intuition and promote overall well-being.

Spiritual and Psychic Benefits

Stress Relief and Calming: Galaxite is renowned for its ability to alleviate stress and anxiety. Its calming energy promotes a sense of peace and tranquility, helping to soothe the mind and body. This makes it an excellent companion for meditation and spiritual practices.

Intuition and Psychic Abilities: Connected to the third eye and crown chakras, Galaxite enhances intuition and psychic abilities. It encourages spiritual insight and clarity, helping individuals connect with their higher self and the universe.

Spiritual Growth: Galaxite is a stone of spiritual growth and evolution. It supports the release of old patterns and facilitates the acceptance of new perspectives, aiding in profound personal transformation.

Enhancement of Healing Energies: Known for its ability to amplify healing energies, Galaxite is used to enhance both personal energy and the effectiveness of other healing crystals. It is beneficial in promoting a balanced and harmonious energy flow during healing sessions.

Harmonization and Balance: Galaxite aids in balancing the body's subtle energies. It aligns the chakras and stabilizes emotions, fostering a harmonious internal environment that supports spiritual and emotional well-being.

Versatile Use in Healing Practices: Utilized in various forms such as raw crystals, jewelry, and meditation tools, Galaxite is a key component in holistic healing practices. It is often used in energy layouts to align and balance the body's energy centers.

Physical Healing Properties

Vitality and Energy: Galaxite is believed to boost physical vitality and energy levels. It helps invigorate the body, enhancing stamina and overall health.

Detoxification: Galaxite aids in detoxifying the body, supporting liver function and cleansing the system of toxins. This contributes to improved metabolic health and overall well-being.

Immune System: Galaxite is believed to enhance the immune system, helping the body fight off illnesses more effectively. It supports the body's natural defenses and promotes overall health and vitality.

Cellular Regeneration: Galaxite supports the body's natural healing processes by promoting cellular regeneration. It aids in the recovery from injuries and illnesses, speeding up the healing process.

Skin Health: Galaxite supports skin health by promoting cellular regeneration and healing. It aids in the treatment of skin conditions and improves the overall appearance of the skin.

Potential Homeopathic Uses

If Galaxite were to be used as a homeopathic remedy, its indications might include:

Psychological Symptoms: Anxiety, emotional stress, and lack of clarity. It may also help in cases of emotional instability and spiritual confusion.

Physical Symptoms: Detoxification needs, immune system deficiencies, and skin conditions.

Behavioral Symptoms: Difficulty in coping with stress, lack of motivation, and a tendency towards emotional imbalance.

Galaxite's homeopathic profile would focus on its ability to transform, protect, and rejuvenate, making it suitable for addressing conditions related to stress, detoxification, and overall well-being.

Conclusion

Galaxite is a vital crystal in holistic healing, celebrated for its mystical beauty and versatile healing properties. Whether used for stress relief, spiritual growth, or as a transformative talisman, Galaxite serves as a potent aid in achieving physical health and spiritual harmony. Like all alternative practices, these should be considered as complementary to conventional medical treatments.

Cerussite: Comprehensive Guide on Spiritual and Physical Healing Properties

Overview

Cerussite, known for its clear to white crystalline appearance, is a unique crystal valued for its grounding and transformative energy. This gemstone is often associated with clarity and adaptability. Cerussite is celebrated for its ability to enhance mental clarity and promote overall well-being.

Spiritual and Psychic Benefits

Stress Relief and Calming: Cerussite is renowned for its ability to alleviate stress and anxiety. Its grounding energy promotes a sense of stability and calm, helping to clear the mind and reduce emotional tension. This makes it an excellent companion for meditation and stress management practices.

Mental Clarity: Connected to the root and crown chakras, Cerussite enhances mental clarity and focus. It encourages clear thinking and decision-making, helping individuals approach challenges with confidence and determination.

Adaptability and Transformation: Cerussite is a stone of adaptability and transformation. It supports personal growth and resilience, helping individuals navigate life changes with grace and ease.

Enhancement of Healing Energies: Known for its ability to amplify healing energies, Cerussite is used to enhance both personal energy and the effectiveness of other healing crystals. It is beneficial in promoting a balanced and harmonious energy flow during healing sessions.

Harmonization and Balance: Cerussite aids in balancing the body's subtle energies. It aligns the chakras and stabilizes emotions, fostering a harmonious internal environment that supports emotional and physical well-being.

Versatile Use in Healing Practices: Utilized in various forms such as raw crystals, jewelry, and meditation tools, Cerussite is a key component in holistic healing practices. It is often used in energy layouts to align and balance the body's energy centers.

Physical Healing Properties

Vitality and Energy: Cerussite is believed to boost physical vitality and energy levels. It helps invigorate the body, enhancing stamina and overall health.

Bone and Joint Health: Cerussite supports bone and joint health, helping to strengthen bones and alleviate joint pain. It is beneficial for those dealing with arthritis and other joint-related issues.

Detoxification: Cerussite aids in detoxifying the body, supporting liver function and cleansing the system of toxins. This contributes to improved metabolic health and overall well-being.

Cellular Regeneration: Cerussite supports the body's natural healing processes by promoting cellular regeneration. It aids in the recovery from injuries and illnesses, speeding up the healing process.

Immune System: Cerussite is believed to enhance the immune system, helping the body to fight off illnesses more effectively. It supports the body's natural defenses and promotes overall health and vitality.

Potential Homeopathic Uses

If Cerussite were to be used as a homeopathic remedy, its indications might include:

Psychological Symptoms: Anxiety, emotional stress, and lack of clarity. It may also help in cases of emotional instability and difficulty adapting to change.

Physical Symptoms: Bone and joint health issues, detoxification needs, and immune system deficiencies.

Behavioral Symptoms: Difficulty in coping with stress, lack of motivation, and a tendency towards emotional imbalance.

Cerussite's homeopathic profile would focus on its ability to ground, protect, and transform, making it suitable for addressing conditions related to stress, bone health, and overall well-being.

Conclusion

Cerussite is a vital crystal in holistic healing, celebrated for its grounding beauty and versatile healing properties. Whether used for stress relief, mental clarity, or as a transformative talisman, Cerussite serves as a potent aid in achieving physical health and spiritual harmony. Like all alternative practices, these should be considered as complementary to conventional medical treatments.

Crocoite: Comprehensive Guide on Spiritual and Physical Healing Properties

Overview

Crocoite, known for its striking bright orange to red crystalline structure, is a rare and powerful crystal valued for its energizing and transformative properties. This gemstone is often associated with passion and vitality. Crocoite is celebrated for its ability to enhance creativity and promote overall well-being.

Spiritual and Psychic Benefits

Stress Relief and Calming: Crocoite is renowned for its ability to alleviate stress and anxiety. Its vibrant energy promotes a sense of joy and enthusiasm, helping to uplift the spirit and dispel negative emotions. This makes it an excellent companion for meditation and stress management practices.

Creativity and Passion: Connected to the sacral chakra, Crocoite enhances creativity and passion. It encourages self-expression and inspires new ideas, making it a powerful tool for artists and creators.

Transformation and Growth: Crocoite is a stone of transformation and growth. It supports the release of old patterns and the acceptance of new perspectives, facilitating profound changes in one's personal and spiritual journey.

Enhancement of Healing Energies: Known for its ability to amplify healing energies, Crocoite is used to enhance both personal energy and the effectiveness of other healing crystals. It is beneficial in promoting a balanced and harmonious energy flow during healing sessions.

Harmonization and Balance: Crocoite aids in balancing the body's subtle energies. It aligns the chakras and stabilizes emotions, fostering a harmonious internal environment that supports emotional and physical well-being.

Versatile Use in Healing Practices: Utilized in various forms such as raw crystals, jewelry, and meditation tools, Crocoite is a key component in holistic healing practices. It is often used in energy layouts to align and balance the body's energy centers.

Physical Healing Properties

Vitality and Energy:

Crocoite is believed to boost physical vitality and energy levels. It helps invigorate the body, enhancing stamina and overall health.

Detoxification: Crocoite aids in detoxifying the body, supporting liver function and cleansing the system of toxins. This contributes to improved metabolic health and overall well-being.

Immune System: Crocoite is believed to enhance the immune system, helping the body to fight off illnesses more effectively. It supports the body's natural defenses and promotes overall health and vitality.

Reproductive Health:Crocoite supports reproductive health, helping to balance hormonal levels and enhance fertility. It is beneficial for those dealing with reproductive issues.

Healing and Regeneration: Crocoite supports the body's natural healing processes by promoting cellular regeneration. It aids in the recovery from injuries and illnesses, speeding up the healing process.

Potential Homeopathic Uses

If Crocoite were to be used as a homeopathic remedy, its indications might include:

Psychological Symptoms: Anxiety, low self-esteem, and lack of motivation. It may also help in cases of emotional instability and lack of passion.

Physical Symptoms: Reproductive health issues, detoxification needs, and immune system deficiencies.

Behavioral Symptoms: Difficulty in coping with stress, lack of creativity, and a tendency towards emotional imbalance.

Crocoite's homeopathic profile would focus on its ability to invigorate, transform, and inspire, making it suitable for addressing conditions related to stress, reproductive health, and overall well-being.

Conclusion

Crocoite is a vital crystal in holistic healing, celebrated for its vibrant beauty and versatile healing properties. Whether used for stress relief, personal empowerment, or as a transformative talisman, Crocoite serves as a potent aid in achieving physical health and spiritual harmony. Like all alternative practices, these should be considered as complementary to conventional medical treatments.

Londonite: Comprehensive Guide on Spiritual and Physical Healing Properties

Overview

Londonite, a rare cesium-rich mineral from the Londonite-Rhodizite series, is known for its vibrant yellow color and powerful metaphysical properties. This gemstone is highly valued for its ability to support emotional healing, enhance mental clarity, and promote spiritual growth.

Spiritual and Psychic Benefits

Spiritual Growth: Londonite is renowned for its ability to enhance spiritual growth and insight. It helps individuals connect with their higher self and spiritual guides, facilitating deeper levels of understanding and awareness.

Emotional Healing: This gemstone aids in emotional healing by releasing negative emotions and past traumas. It promotes inner peace and emotional balance, making it easier to navigate life's challenges.

Intuition and Psychic Abilities: Londonite is known to enhance intuitive abilities and psychic awareness. It opens the solar plexus and crown chakras, facilitating a stronger connection to higher realms and deeper states of consciousness.

Clarity and Focus: Londonite enhances mental clarity and focus. It helps clear mental fog and improve concentration, making it an excellent stone for students and professionals.

Manifestation: Known for its ability to amplify intentions and desires, Londonite is often used as a manifestation tool to attract and achieve one's goals and dreams.

Physical Healing Properties

Immune System Support: Londonite is believed to boost the immune system, helping the body fight off infections and illnesses more effectively. It supports overall health and vitality.

Pain Relief: This gemstone is known to provide relief from physical pain, particularly for conditions related to inflammation and muscle

tension. It helps reduce discomfort and promote overall physical well-being.

Detoxification: Londonite aids in the detoxification process, supporting the body's natural ability to eliminate toxins. It enhances liver and kidney function, promoting overall metabolic health.

Cellular Regeneration: Londonite is known to support cellular regeneration and healing. It aids in the repair of tissues and can be beneficial in the recovery process from injuries and surgeries.

Stress Relief: Known for its calming properties, Londonite helps reduce stress and anxiety. It provides a soothing energy that helps balance emotions and promote a sense of peace and well-being.

Potential Homeopathic Uses

If Londonite were to be used as a homeopathic remedy, its indications might include:

Psychological Symptoms: Anxiety, stress, emotional trauma, and lack of manifestation. It may also help with issues related to intuition and clarity.

Physical Symptoms: Immune system deficiencies, pain relief, detoxification needs, and cellular regeneration.

Behavioral Symptoms: Difficulty in managing stress, lack of focus during intellectual tasks, and challenges in emotional healing.

Londonite's homeopathic profile would focus on its ability to heal, manifest, and clarify, making it suitable for addressing conditions related to stress, energy depletion, and emotional trauma.

Conclusion

Londonite is a powerful gemstone that offers a multitude of benefits for both physical and spiritual well-being. Its ability to enhance mental clarity, support emotional healing, and promote overall health makes it a valuable tool in holistic healing practices. Whether used in meditation, as a manifestation talisman, or for its physical healing properties, Londonite stands out as a gem of clarity and empowerment.

As with all alternative practices, these should complement conventional medical treatments and be used responsibly.

Muscovite: Comprehensive Guide on Spiritual and Physical Healing Properties

Overview

Muscovite, a common mica mineral with a pearly luster and a range of colors from clear to shades of green, pink, and yellow, is known for its powerful metaphysical properties. This gemstone is highly valued for its ability to support emotional healing, enhance mental clarity, and promote spiritual growth.

Spiritual and Psychic Benefits

Spiritual Growth: Muscovite is renowned for its ability to enhance spiritual growth and insight. It helps individuals connect with their higher self and spiritual guides, facilitating deeper levels of understanding and awareness.

Emotional Healing: This gemstone aids in emotional healing by releasing negative emotions and past traumas. It promotes inner peace and emotional balance, making it easier to navigate life's challenges.

Intuition and Psychic Abilities: Muscovite is known to enhance intuitive abilities and psychic awareness. It opens the heart and third eye chakras, facilitating a stronger connection to higher realms and deeper states of consciousness.

Clarity and Focus: Muscovite enhances mental clarity and focus. It helps clear mental fog and improve concentration, making it an excellent stone for students and professionals.

Self-Reflection: Known for its ability to promote self-reflection, Muscovite helps individuals gain insight into their own behaviors and patterns, fostering personal growth and self-improvement.

Physical Healing Properties

Immune System Support: Muscovite is believed to boost the immune system, helping the body to fight off infections and illnesses more effectively. It supports overall health and vitality.

Pain Relief: This gemstone is known to provide relief from physical pain, particularly for conditions related to inflammation and muscle

tension. It helps reduce discomfort and promote overall physical well-being.

Detoxification: Muscovite aids in the detoxification process, supporting the body's natural ability to eliminate toxins. It enhances liver and kidney function, promoting overall metabolic health.

Cellular Regeneration: Muscovite is known to support cellular regeneration and healing. It aids in the repair of tissues and can be beneficial in the recovery process from injuries and surgeries.

Stress Relief: Known for its calming properties, Muscovite helps reduce stress and anxiety. It provides a soothing energy that helps balance emotions and promote a sense of peace and well-being.

Potential Homeopathic Uses

If Muscovite were to be used as a homeopathic remedy, its indications might include:

Psychological Symptoms: Anxiety, stress, emotional trauma, and lack of self-reflection. It may also help with issues related to intuition and clarity.

Physical Symptoms: Immune system deficiencies, pain relief, detoxification needs, and cellular regeneration.

Behavioral Symptoms: Difficulty in managing stress, lack of focus during intellectual tasks, and challenges in emotional healing.

Muscovite's homeopathic profile would focus on its ability to heal, clarify, and empower, making it suitable for addressing conditions related to stress, energy depletion, and emotional trauma.

Conclusion

Muscovite is a powerful gemstone that offers a multitude of benefits for both physical and spiritual well-being. Its ability to enhance mental clarity, support emotional healing, and promote overall health makes it a valuable tool in holistic healing practices. Whether used in meditation, as a self-reflection talisman, or for its physical healing properties, Muscovite stands out as a gem of clarity and empowerment.

As with all alternative practices, these should complement conventional medical treatments and be used responsibly.

Petalite: Comprehensive Guide on Spiritual and Physical Healing Properties

Overview

Petalite, a lithium aluminum phyllosilicate mineral, is known for its soft pink to clear

color and powerful healing properties. This gemstone is highly valued for its ability to support emotional healing, enhance mental clarity, and promote spiritual growth.

Spiritual and Psychic Benefits

Spiritual Growth: Petalite is renowned for its ability to enhance spiritual growth and insight. It helps individuals connect with their higher self and spiritual guides, facilitating deeper levels of understanding and awareness.

Emotional Healing: This gemstone aids in emotional healing by releasing negative emotions and past traumas. It promotes inner peace and emotional balance, making it easier to navigate life's challenges.

Intuition and Psychic Abilities: Petalite is known to enhance intuitive abilities and psychic awareness. It opens the heart and crown chakras, facilitating a stronger connection to higher realms and deeper states of consciousness.

Clarity and Focus: Petalite enhances mental clarity and focus. It helps clear mental fog and improve concentration, making it an excellent stone for students and professionals.

Calming and Soothing: Known for its calming and soothing qualities, Petalite helps reduce stress and anxiety, promoting a sense of peace and relaxation.

Physical Healing Properties

Immune System Support: Petalite is believed to boost the immune system, helping the body fight off infections and illnesses more effectively. It supports overall health and vitality.

Pain Relief: This gemstone is known to provide relief from physical pain, particularly for conditions related to inflammation and muscle

tension. It helps reduce discomfort and promote overall physical well-being.

Detoxification: Petalite aids in the detoxification process, supporting the body's natural ability to eliminate toxins. It enhances liver and kidney function, promoting overall metabolic health.

Cellular Regeneration: Petalite is known to support cellular regeneration and healing. It aids in the repair of tissues and can be beneficial in the recovery process from injuries and surgeries.

Stress Relief: Known for its calming properties, Petalite helps reduce stress and anxiety. It provides a soothing energy that helps balance emotions and promote a sense of peace and well-being.

Potential Homeopathic Uses

If Petalite were to be used as a homeopathic remedy, its indications might include:

Psychological Symptoms: Anxiety, stress, emotional trauma, and lack of calm. It may also help with issues related to intuition and clarity.

-mPhysical Symptoms: Immune system deficiencies, pain relief, detoxification needs, and cellular regeneration.

Behavioral Symptoms: Difficulty in managing stress, lack of focus during calming tasks, and challenges in emotional healing.

Petalite's homeopathic profile would focus on its ability to heal, calm, and clarify, making it suitable for addressing conditions related to stress, energy depletion, and emotional trauma.

Conclusion

Petalite is a powerful gemstone that offers a multitude of benefits for both physical and spiritual well-being. Its ability to enhance mental clarity, support emotional healing, and promote overall health makes it a valuable tool in holistic healing practices. Whether used in meditation, as a calming talisman, or for its physical healing properties, Petalite stands out as a gem of tranquility and healing. As with all alternative practices, these should complement conventional medical treatments and be used responsibly.

Roselite: Comprehensive Guide on Spiritual and Physical Healing Properties

Overview

Roselite, a rare calcium cobalt arsenate mineral, is known for its striking rose-red color and powerful healing properties. This gemstone is highly valued for its ability to support emotional healing, enhance mental clarity, and promote spiritual growth.

Spiritual and Psychic Benefits

Spiritual Growth: Roselite is renowned for its ability to enhance spiritual growth and insight. It helps individuals connect with their higher self and spiritual guides, facilitating deeper levels of understanding and awareness.

Emotional Healing: This gemstone aids in emotional healing by releasing negative emotions and past traumas. It promotes inner peace and emotional balance, making it easier to navigate life's challenges.

Intuition and Psychic Abilities: Roselite is known to enhance intuitive abilities and psychic awareness. It opens the heart and crown chakras, facilitating a stronger connection to higher realms and deeper states of consciousness.

Clarity and Focus: Roselite enhances mental clarity and focus. It helps clear mental fog and improve concentration, making it an excellent stone for students and professionals.

Joy and Optimism: Known for its ability to promote joy and optimism, Roselite raises the vibration of the surrounding environment, encouraging feelings of happiness and overall well-being.

Physical Healing Properties

Immune System Support: Roselite is believed to boost the immune system, helping the body fight off infections and illnesses more effectively. It supports overall health and vitality.

Pain Relief: This gemstone is known to provide relief from physical pain, particularly for conditions related to inflammation and muscle

tension. It helps reduce discomfort and promote overall physical well-being.

Detoxification: Roselite aids in the detoxification process, supporting the body's natural ability to eliminate toxins. It enhances liver and kidney function, promoting overall metabolic health.

Cellular Regeneration: Roselite is known to support cellular regeneration and healing. It aids in the repair of tissues and can be beneficial in the recovery process from injuries and surgeries.

Stress Relief: Known for its calming properties, Roselite helps reduce stress and anxiety. It provides a soothing energy that helps balance emotions and promote a sense of peace and well-being.

Potential Homeopathic Uses

If Roselite were to be used as a homeopathic remedy, its indications might include:

Psychological Symptoms: Anxiety, stress, emotional trauma, and lack of joy. It may also help with issues related to intuition and clarity.

Physical Symptoms: Immune system deficiencies, pain relief, detoxification needs, and cellular regeneration.

Behavioral Symptoms: Difficulty in managing stress, lack of focus during joyful tasks, and challenges in emotional healing.

Roselite's homeopathic profile would focus on its ability to heal, uplift, and clarify, making it suitable for addressing conditions related to stress, energy depletion, and emotional trauma.

Conclusion

Roselite is a powerful gemstone that offers a multitude of benefits for both physical and spiritual well-being. Its ability to enhance mental clarity, support emotional healing, and promote overall health makes it a valuable tool in holistic healing practices. Whether used in meditation, as an uplifting talisman, or for its physical healing properties, Roselite stands out as a gem of joy and healing. As with all alternative practices, these should complement conventional medical treatments and be used responsibly.

Siderite: Comprehensive Guide on Spiritual and Physical Healing Properties

Overview

Siderite, a carbonate mineral of iron, is known for its earthy brown to yellowish-brown color and its powerful healing properties. This gemstone is highly valued for its grounding and stabilizing qualities, as well as its ability to support emotional healing, enhance mental clarity, and promote spiritual growth.

Spiritual and Psychic Benefits

Grounding and Stability: Siderite is renowned for its grounding and stabilizing qualities. It helps anchor energy and provide a sense of stability and security, making it an excellent stone for those who feel scattered or disconnected.

Emotional Healing: This gemstone aids in emotional healing by releasing negative emotions and past traumas. It promotes inner peace and emotional balance, making it easier to navigate life's challenges.

Spiritual Growth: Siderite enhances spiritual growth and insight. It helps individuals connect with their higher self and spiritual guides, facilitating deeper levels of understanding and awareness.

Clarity and Focus: Siderite enhances mental clarity and focus. It helps clear mental fog and improve concentration, making it an excellent stone for students and professionals.

Strength and Resilience: Known for its ability to foster strength and resilience, Siderite helps individuals overcome challenges and maintain focus and determination.

Physical Healing Properties

Immune System Support: Siderite is believed to boost the immune system, helping the body fight off infections and illnesses more effectively. It supports overall health and vitality.

Pain Relief: This gemstone is known to provide relief from physical pain, particularly for conditions related to inflammation and muscle

tension. It helps reduce discomfort and promote overall physical well-being.

Detoxification: Siderite aids in the detoxification process, supporting the body's natural ability to eliminate toxins. It enhances liver and kidney function, promoting overall metabolic health.

Cellular Regeneration: Siderite is known to support cellular regeneration and healing. It aids in the repair of tissues and can be beneficial in the recovery process from injuries and surgeries.

Stress Relief: Known for its calming properties, Siderite helps reduce stress and anxiety. It provides a soothing energy that helps balance emotions and promote a sense of peace and well-being.

Potential Homeopathic Uses

If Siderite were to be used as a homeopathic remedy, its indications might include:

Psychological Symptoms: Anxiety, stress, emotional trauma, and lack of grounding. It may also help with issues related to strength and resilience.

Physical Symptoms: Immune system deficiencies, pain relief, detoxification needs, and cellular regeneration.

Behavioral Symptoms: Difficulty in managing stress, lack of focus during grounding tasks, and challenges in emotional healing.

Siderite's homeopathic profile would focus on its ability to ground, heal, and strengthen, making it suitable for addressing conditions related to stress, energy depletion, and emotional trauma.

Conclusion

Siderite is a powerful gemstone that offers a multitude of benefits for both physical and spiritual well-being. Its ability to enhance mental clarity, support emotional healing, and promote overall health makes it a valuable tool in holistic healing practices. Whether used in meditation, as a grounding talisman, or for its physical healing properties, Siderite stands out as a gem of stability and strength. As with all alternative practices, these should complement conventional medical treatments and be used responsibly.

Anhydrite: Comprehensive Guide on Spiritual and Physical Healing Properties

Overview

Anhydrite, a sulfate mineral commonly found in evaporite deposits, is known for its delicate blue and white colors and its powerful healing properties. This gemstone is highly valued for its ability to support emotional healing, enhance mental clarity, and promote spiritual growth.

Spiritual and Psychic Benefits

Emotional Healing: Anhydrite is renowned for its ability to support emotional healing. It helps individuals release negative emotions and past traumas, promoting a sense of peace and emotional balance.

Spiritual Awareness: This gemstone enhances spiritual growth by promoting awareness and understanding of one's spiritual path. It helps individuals connect with their higher self and spiritual guides.

Calm and Serenity: Anhydrite promotes a calm and serene state of mind. It helps to reduce stress and anxiety, making it easier to achieve a peaceful and meditative state.

Communication: Known for its ability to enhance communication, Anhydrite helps individuals express themselves more clearly and effectively. It supports both verbal and non-verbal communication.

Intuition: Anhydrite enhances intuitive abilities and psychic awareness. It helps individuals trust their instincts and develop a deeper understanding of their inner guidance.

Physical Healing Properties

Bone and Joint Health: Anhydrite is believed to support the health of bones and joints. It helps to strengthen the skeletal system and alleviate conditions related to bone and joint issues.

Detoxification: This gemstone aids in the detoxification process, supporting the body's natural ability to eliminate toxins and improve overall health.

Pain Relief: Anhydrite is known to provide relief from physical pain, particularly for conditions related to inflammation and muscle tension.

Respiratory Health: Anhydrite supports respiratory health, helping to alleviate conditions related to the lungs and breathing.

Metabolic Balance: Anhydrite aids in balancing metabolic functions, supporting overall physical health and vitality.

Potential Homeopathic Uses

If Anhydrite were to be used as a homeopathic remedy, its indications might include:

Psychological Symptoms: Emotional trauma, stress, anxiety, and difficulty in communication. It may also help with issues related to intuition.

Physical Symptoms: Bone and joint health issues, detoxification needs, pain relief, and respiratory conditions.

Behavioral Symptoms: Difficulty expressing oneself, lack of calm, and challenges in emotional regulation.

Anhydrite's homeopathic profile would focus on its ability to heal, calm, and clarify, making it suitable for addressing conditions related to stress, energy depletion, and emotional trauma.

Conclusion

Anhydrite is a powerful gemstone that offers a multitude of benefits for both physical and spiritual well-being. Its ability to support emotional healing, enhance communication, and promote overall health makes it a valuable tool in holistic healing practices. Whether used in meditation, as a calming talisman, or for its physical healing properties, Anhydrite stands out as a gem of serenity and healing. As with all alternative practices, these should complement conventional medical treatments and be used responsibly.

Atacamite: Comprehensive Guide on Spiritual and Physical Healing Properties

Overview

Atacamite, a copper chloride hydroxide mineral, is known for its vivid green color and powerful healing properties. This gemstone is highly valued for its ability to support emotional healing, enhance mental clarity, and promote spiritual growth.

Spiritual and Psychic Benefits

Spiritual Growth: Atacamite is renowned for its ability to enhance spiritual growth and insight. It helps individuals connect with their higher self and spiritual guides, facilitating deeper levels of understanding and awareness.

Emotional Healing: This gemstone aids in emotional healing by helping to release negative emotions and past traumas. It promotes a sense of calm and emotional balance, making it easier to navigate life's challenges.

Intuition and Psychic Abilities: Atacamite is known to enhance intuitive abilities and psychic awareness. It opens the heart and third eye chakras, facilitating a stronger connection to higher realms and deeper states of consciousness.

Clarity and Focus: Atacamite enhances mental clarity and focus. It helps to clear mental fog and improve concentration, making it an excellent stone for students and professionals.

Courage and Confidence: Known for its ability to foster courage and confidence, Atacamite helps individuals overcome challenges and maintain focus and determination.

Physical Healing Properties

Immune System Support: Atacamite is believed to boost the immune system, helping the body to fight off infections and illnesses more effectively. It supports overall health and vitality.

Pain Relief: This gemstone is known to provide relief from physical pain, particularly for conditions related to inflammation and muscle

tension. It helps to reduce discomfort and promote overall physical well-being.

Detoxification: Atacamite aids in the detoxification process, supporting the body's natural ability to eliminate toxins. It enhances liver and kidney function, promoting overall metabolic health.

Cellular Regeneration: Atacamite is known to support cellular regeneration and healing. It aids in the repair of tissues and can be beneficial in the recovery process from injuries and surgeries.

Stress Relief: Known for its calming properties, Atacamite helps to reduce stress and anxiety. It provides a soothing energy that helps to balance emotions and promote a sense of peace and well-being.

Potential Homeopathic Uses

If Atacamite were to be used as a homeopathic remedy, its indications might include:

Psychological Symptoms: Anxiety, stress, emotional trauma, and lack of courage. It may also help with issues related to intuition and clarity.

Physical Symptoms: Immune system deficiencies, pain relief, detoxification needs, and cellular regeneration.

Behavioral Symptoms: Difficulty in managing stress, lack of focus during intellectual tasks, and challenges in emotional healing.

Atacamite's homeopathic profile would focus on its ability to heal, clarify, and empower, making it suitable for addressing conditions related to stress, energy depletion, and emotional trauma.

Conclusion

Atacamite is a powerful gemstone that offers a multitude of benefits for both physical and spiritual well-being. Its ability to enhance mental clarity, support emotional healing, and promote overall health makes it a valuable tool in holistic healing practices. Whether used in meditation, as a courage talisman, or for its physical healing properties, Atacamite stands out as a gem of clarity and empowerment. As with all alternative practices, these should complement conventional medical treatments and be used responsibly.

Bastnasite: Comprehensive Guide on Spiritual and Physical Healing Properties

Overview

Bastnasite, a rare earth carbonate mineral, is known for its honey-yellow to reddish-brown color and powerful healing properties. This gemstone is highly valued for its ability to support emotional healing, enhance mental clarity, and promote spiritual growth.

Spiritual and Psychic Benefits

Spiritual Growth: Bastnasite is renowned for its ability to enhance spiritual growth and insight. It helps individuals connect with their higher self and spiritual guides, facilitating deeper levels of understanding and awareness.

Emotional Healing: This gemstone aids in emotional healing by helping to release negative emotions and past traumas. It promotes a sense of calm and emotional balance, making it easier to navigate life's challenges.

Intuition and Psychic Abilities: Bastnasite is known to enhance intuitive abilities and psychic awareness. It opens the heart and third eye chakras, facilitating a stronger connection to higher realms and deeper states of consciousness.

Clarity and Focus: Bastnasite enhances mental clarity and focus. It helps to clear mental fog and improve concentration, making it an excellent stone for students and professionals.

Energy and Motivation: Known for its ability to boost energy and motivation, Bastnasite helps individuals stay focused and driven, supporting the pursuit of goals and ambitions.

Physical Healing Properties

Immune System Support: Bastnasite is believed to boost the immune system, helping the body to fight off infections and illnesses more effectively. It supports overall health and vitality.

Pain Relief: This gemstone is known to provide relief from physical pain, particularly for conditions related to inflammation and muscle tension. It helps to reduce discomfort and promote overall physical well-being.

Detoxification: Bastnasite aids in the detoxification process, supporting the body's natural ability to eliminate toxins. It enhances liver and kidney function, promoting overall metabolic health.

Cellular Regeneration: Bastnasite is known to support cellular regeneration and healing. It aids in the repair of tissues and can be beneficial in the recovery process from injuries and surgeries.

Stress Relief: Known for its calming properties, Bastnasite helps to reduce stress and anxiety. It provides a soothing energy that helps to balance emotions and promote a sense of peace and well-being.

Potential Homeopathic Uses

If Bastnasite were to be used as a homeopathic remedy, its indications might include:

Psychological Symptoms: Anxiety, stress, emotional trauma, and lack of motivation. It may also help with issues related to intuition and clarity.

Physical Symptoms: Immune system deficiencies, pain relief, detoxification needs, and cellular regeneration.

Behavioral Symptoms: Difficulty in managing stress, lack of focus during intellectual tasks, and challenges in emotional healing.

Bastnasite's homeopathic profile would focus on its ability to heal, energize, and clarify, making it suitable for addressing conditions related to stress, energy depletion, and emotional trauma.

Conclusion

Bastnasite is a powerful gemstone that offers a multitude of benefits for both physical and spiritual well-being. Its ability to enhance mental clarity, support emotional healing, and promote overall health makes it a valuable tool in holistic healing practices. Whether used in meditation, as a motivation talisman, or for its physical healing properties, Bastnasite stands out as a gem of clarity and energy. As with all alternative practices, these should complement conventional medical treatments and be used responsibly.

Colemanite: Comprehensive Guide on Spiritual and Physical Healing Properties

Overview

Colemanite, a borate mineral known for its clear to white crystalline appearance, is celebrated for its powerful healing properties. This gemstone is highly valued for its ability to support emotional healing, enhance mental clarity, and promote spiritual growth.

Spiritual and Psychic Benefits

Spiritual Growth: Colemanite is renowned for its ability to enhance spiritual growth and insight. It helps individuals connect with their higher self and spiritual guides, facilitating deeper levels of understanding and awareness.

Emotional Healing: This gemstone aids in emotional healing by helping to release negative emotions and past traumas. It promotes a sense of calm and emotional balance, making it easier to navigate life's challenges.

Intuition and Psychic Abilities: Colemanite is known to enhance intuitive abilities and psychic awareness. It opens the third eye and crown chakras, facilitating a stronger connection to higher realms and deeper states of consciousness.

Clarity and Focus: Colemanite enhances mental clarity and focus. It helps to clear mental fog and improve concentration, making it an excellent stone for students and professionals.

Problem Solving: Known for its ability to aid in problem-solving, Colemanite helps individuals assess situations with clarity and make informed decisions.

Physical Healing Properties

Immune System Support: Colemanite is believed to boost the immune system, helping the body to fight off infections and illnesses more effectively. It supports overall health and vitality.

Pain Relief: This gemstone is known to provide relief from physical pain, particularly for conditions related to inflammation and muscle tension. It helps to reduce discomfort and promote overall physical well-being.

Detoxification: Colemanite aids in the detoxification process, supporting the body's natural ability to eliminate toxins. It enhances liver and kidney function, promoting overall metabolic health.

Cellular Regeneration: Colemanite is known to support cellular regeneration and healing. It aids in the repair of tissues and can be beneficial in the recovery process from injuries and surgeries.

Stress Relief: Known for its calming properties, Colemanite helps to reduce stress and anxiety. It provides a soothing energy that helps to balance emotions and promote a sense of peace and well-being.

Potential Homeopathic Uses

If Colemanite were to be used as a homeopathic remedy, its indications might include:

Psychological Symptoms: Anxiety, stress, emotional trauma, and difficulty in problem-solving. It may also help with issues related to intuition and clarity.

Physical Symptoms: Immune system deficiencies, pain relief, detoxification needs, and cellular regeneration.

Behavioral Symptoms: Difficulty managing stress, lack of focus during intellectual tasks, and challenges in emotional healing.

Colemanite's homeopathic profile would focus on its ability to heal, clarify, and solve, making it suitable for addressing conditions related to stress, energy depletion, and emotional trauma.

Conclusion

Colemanite is a powerful gemstone that offers a multitude of benefits for both physical and spiritual well-being. Its ability to enhance mental clarity, support emotional healing, and promote overall health makes it a valuable tool in holistic healing practices. Whether used in meditation, as a problem-solving talisman, or for its physical healing properties, Colemanite stands out as a gem of clarity and healing. As with all alternative practices, these should complement conventional medical treatments and be used responsibly.

Anorthite: Comprehensive Guide on Spiritual and Physical Healing Properties

Overview

Anorthite, a member of the plagioclase feldspar group, is typically found in colors ranging from white to grey. This gemstone is highly valued for its grounding energy and its ability to enhance mental clarity and emotional stability. Anorthite is known for its protective and stabilizing qualities.

Spiritual and Psychic Benefits

Grounding and Stability: Anorthite is renowned for its strong grounding properties. It helps individuals stay connected to their physical bodies and the Earth, providing a sense of stability and security.

Mental Clarity: This gemstone enhances mental clarity and focus. It helps to clear mental fog and improve concentration, making it an excellent stone for students and professionals.

Emotional Stability: Anorthite aids in emotional stability by helping to release negative emotions and past traumas. It promotes a sense of calm and emotional balance, making it easier to navigate life's challenges.

Protection: Known for its protective properties, Anorthite helps to shield the wearer from negative influences. It also has grounding properties that help individuals stay connected to their physical bodies and the Earth.

Spiritual Insight: Anorthite enhances spiritual insight and intuition. It opens the third eye and crown chakras, facilitating deeper connections to higher realms and spiritual guides.

Physical Healing Properties

Bone Health: Anorthite is believed to benefit bone health, enhancing the strength and density of bones. It supports overall skeletal health.

Digestive Health: This gemstone supports digestive health and improves metabolism. It helps to regulate the digestive system and alleviate issues such as indigestion and stomach discomfort.

Immune System Boost: Anorthite is thought to boost the immune system, helping the body to fight off infections and illnesses more effectively. It supports overall health and vitality.

Pain Relief: Anorthite is known to provide relief from physical pain, particularly for conditions related to inflammation and muscle tension. It helps to reduce discomfort and promote overall physical well-being.

Stress Relief: Known for its calming properties, Anorthite helps to reduce stress and anxiety. It provides a soothing energy that helps to balance emotions and promote a sense of peace and well-being.

Potential Homeopathic Uses

If Anorthite were to be used as a homeopathic remedy, its indications might include:

Psychological Symptoms: Emotional instability, stress, and difficulty in managing emotions.

Physical Symptoms: Bone health concerns, digestive issues, immune deficiencies, and pain relief.

Behavioral Symptoms: Challenges in maintaining focus, lack of emotional balance, and difficulties in managing stress.

Anorthite's homeopathic profile would focus on its ability to heal, ground, and stabilize, making it suitable for addressing conditions related to emotional stability, mental clarity, and overall health.

Conclusion

Anorthite is a versatile gemstone that offers a range of benefits for both physical and spiritual well-being. Its ability to enhance mental clarity, support emotional stability, and promote overall health makes it a valuable tool in holistic healing practices. Whether used in meditation, as a grounding talisman, or for its physical healing properties, Anorthite stands out as a gem of stability and vitality. As with all alternative practices, these should complement conventional medical treatments and be used responsibly.

Arfvedsonite: Comprehensive Guide on Spiritual and Physical Healing Properties

Overview

Arfvedsonite is a rare and striking mineral that typically exhibits a dark blue to black color with a shimmering appearance. This gemstone is highly valued for its unique energy, which is believed to promote spiritual growth, mental clarity, and emotional healing.

Spiritual and Psychic Benefits

Spiritual Growth: Arfvedsonite is renowned for its ability to enhance spiritual growth and insight. It helps individuals connect with their higher self and spiritual guides, facilitating deeper levels of understanding and awareness.

Mental Clarity: This gemstone enhances mental clarity and focus. It helps to clear mental fog and improve concentration, making it an excellent stone for students and professionals.

Emotional Healing: Arfvedsonite aids in emotional healing by helping to release negative emotions and past traumas. It promotes a sense of calm and emotional balance, making it easier to navigate life's challenges.

Intuition and Insight: Arfvedsonite enhances intuitive abilities and spiritual insight. It opens the third eye and crown chakras, facilitating deeper connections to higher realms and spiritual guides.

Protection: Known for its protective properties, Arfvedsonite helps to shield the wearer from negative influences. It also has grounding properties that help individuals stay connected to their physical bodies and the Earth.

Physical Healing Properties

Nervous System Support: Arfvedsonite is believed to support the nervous system, enhancing its function and reducing stress and anxiety. It promotes overall mental well-being.

Detoxification: This gemstone aids in the detoxification process, supporting the body's natural ability to eliminate toxins. It enhances liver and kidney function, promoting overall metabolic health.

Immune System Boost: Arfvedsonite is thought to boost the immune system, helping the body to fight off infections and illnesses more effectively. It supports overall health and vitality.

Pain Relief: Arfvedsonite is known to provide relief from physical pain, particularly for conditions related to inflammation and muscle tension. It helps to reduce discomfort and promote overall physical well-being.

Cellular Regeneration: Arfvedsonite supports cellular regeneration and healing. It aids in the repair of tissues and can be beneficial in the recovery process from injuries and surgeries.

Potential Homeopathic Uses

If Arfvedsonite were to be used as a homeopathic remedy, its indications might include:

Psychological Symptoms: Mental fog, emotional instability, stress, and difficulty in spiritual connection.

Physical Symptoms: Nervous system support, detoxification needs, immune deficiencies, and pain relief.

Behavioral Symptoms: Challenges in maintaining focus, lack of emotional balance, and difficulties in managing stress.

Arfvedsonite's homeopathic profile would focus on its ability to heal, protect, and clarify, making it suitable for addressing conditions related to mental clarity, emotional healing, and overall vitality.

Conclusion

Arfvedsonite is a rare and powerful gemstone that offers a multitude of benefits for both physical and spiritual well-being. Its ability to enhance mental clarity, support emotional healing, and promote overall health makes it a valuable tool in holistic healing practices. Whether used in meditation, as a protective talisman, or for its physical healing properties, Arfvedsonite stands out as a gem of clarity and vitality. As with all alternative practices, these should complement conventional medical treatments and be used responsibly.

Aurichalcite: Comprehensive Guide on Spiritual and Physical Healing Properties

Overview

Aurichalcite is a beautiful and rare mineral that typically exhibits a vibrant blue-green color. This gemstone is highly valued for its unique energy, which is believed to promote mental clarity, emotional healing, and spiritual growth.

Spiritual and Psychic Benefits

Spiritual Growth: Aurichalcite is renowned for its ability to enhance spiritual growth and insight. It helps individuals connect with their higher self and spiritual guides, facilitating deeper levels of understanding and awareness.

Mental Clarity: This gemstone enhances mental clarity and focus. It helps to clear mental fog and improve concentration, making it an excellent stone for students and professionals.

Emotional Healing: Aurichalcite aids in emotional healing by helping to release negative emotions and past traumas. It promotes a sense of calm and emotional balance, making it easier to navigate life's challenges.

Intuition and Insight: Aurichalcite enhances intuitive abilities and spiritual insight. It opens the third eye and crown chakras, facilitating deeper connections to higher realms and spiritual guides.

Protection: Known for its protective properties, Aurichalcite helps to shield the wearer from negative influences. It also has grounding properties that help individuals stay connected to their physical bodies and the Earth.

Physical Healing Properties

Nervous System Support: Aurichalcite is believed to support the nervous system, enhancing its function and reducing stress and anxiety. It promotes overall mental well-being.

Detoxification: This gemstone aids in the detoxification process, supporting the body's natural ability to eliminate toxins. It enhances liver and kidney function, promoting overall metabolic health.

Immune System Boost: Aurichalcite is thought to boost the immune system, helping the body to fight off infections and illnesses more effectively. It supports overall health and vitality.

Pain Relief: Aurichalcite is known to provide relief from physical pain, particularly for conditions related to inflammation and muscle tension. It helps to reduce discomfort and promote overall physical well-being.

Cellular Regeneration: Aurichalcite supports cellular regeneration and healing. It aids in the repair of tissues and can be beneficial in the recovery process from injuries and surgeries.

Potential Homeopathic Uses

If Aurichalcite were to be used as a homeopathic remedy, its indications might include:

Psychological Symptoms: Mental fog, emotional instability, stress, and difficulty in spiritual connection.

Physical Symptoms: Nervous system support, detoxification needs, immune deficiencies, and pain relief.

Behavioral Symptoms: Challenges in maintaining focus, lack of emotional balance, and difficulties in managing stress.

Aurichalcite's homeopathic profile would focus on its ability to heal, protect, and clarify, making it suitable for addressing conditions related to mental clarity, emotional healing, and overall vitality.

Conclusion

Aurichalcite is a rare and powerful gemstone that offers a multitude of benefits for both physical and spiritual well-being. Its ability to enhance mental clarity, support emotional healing, and promote overall health makes it a valuable tool in holistic healing practices. Whether used in meditation, as a protective talisman, or for its physical healing properties, Aurichalcite stands out as a gem of clarity and vitality. As with all alternative practices, these should complement conventional medical treatments and be used responsibly.

Bustamite: Comprehensive Guide on Spiritual and Physical Healing Properties

Overview

Bustamite is a rare and beautiful mineral that typically exhibits colors ranging from pink to brown. This gemstone is highly valued for its unique energy, which is believed to promote emotional healing, mental clarity, and spiritual growth.

Spiritual and Psychic Benefits

Emotional Healing: Bustamite is renowned for its ability to facilitate emotional healing. It helps individuals to release negative emotions and past traumas, promoting a sense of calm and emotional balance.

Mental Clarity: This gemstone enhances mental clarity and focus. It helps to clear mental fog and improve concentration, making it an excellent stone for students and professionals.

Spiritual Growth: Bustamite enhances spiritual growth and insight. It helps individuals connect with their higher self and spiritual guides, facilitating deeper levels of understanding and awareness.

Intuition and Insight: Bustamite enhances intuitive abilities and spiritual insight. It opens the third eye and crown chakras, facilitating deeper connections to higher realms and spiritual guides.

Protection: Known for its protective properties, Bustamite helps to shield the wearer from negative influences. It also has grounding properties that help individuals stay connected to their physical bodies and the Earth.

Physical Healing Properties

Nervous System Support: Bustamite is believed to support the nervous system, enhancing its function and reducing stress and anxiety. It promotes overall mental well-being.

Detoxification: This gemstone aids in the detoxification process, supporting the body's natural ability to eliminate toxins. It enhances liver and kidney function, promoting overall metabolic health.

Immune System Boost: Bustamite is thought to boost the immune system, helping the body to fight off infections and illnesses more effectively. It supports overall health and vitality.

Pain Relief: Bustamite is known to provide relief from physical pain, particularly for conditions related to inflammation and muscle tension. It helps to reduce discomfort and promote overall physical well-being.

Cellular Regeneration: Bustamite supports cellular regeneration and healing. It aids in the repair of tissues and can be beneficial in the recovery process from injuries and surgeries.

Potential Homeopathic Uses

If Bustamite were to be used as a homeopathic remedy, its indications might include:

Psychological Symptoms: Mental fog, emotional instability, stress, and difficulty in spiritual connection.

Physical Symptoms: Nervous system support, detoxification needs, immune deficiencies, and pain relief.

Behavioral Symptoms: Challenges in maintaining focus, lack of emotional balance, and difficulties in managing stress.

Bustamite's homeopathic profile would focus on its ability to heal, protect, and clarify, making it suitable for addressing conditions related to mental clarity, emotional healing, and overall vitality.

Conclusion

Bustamite is a rare and powerful gemstone that offers a multitude of benefits for both physical and spiritual well-being. Its ability to enhance mental clarity, support emotional healing, and promote overall health makes it a valuable tool in holistic healing practices. Whether used in meditation, as a protective talisman, or for its physical healing properties, Bustamite stands out as a gem of clarity and vitality. As with all alternative practices, these should complement conventional medical treatments and be used responsibly.

Celestobarite: Comprehensive Guide on Spiritual and Physical Healing Properties

Overview

Celestobarite is a unique and striking mineral that typically exhibits a combination of blue, white, and grey colors. This gemstone is highly valued for its unique energy, which is believed to promote spiritual growth, emotional healing, and mental clarity.

Spiritual and Psychic Benefits

Spiritual Growth: Celestobarite is renowned for its ability to enhance spiritual growth and insight. It helps individuals connect with their higher self and spiritual guides, facilitating deeper levels of understanding and awareness.

Emotional Healing: This gemstone aids in emotional healing by helping to release negative emotions and past traumas. It promotes a sense of calm and emotional balance, making it easier to navigate life's challenges.

Mental Clarity: Celestobarite enhances mental clarity and focus. It helps to clear mental fog and improve concentration, making it an excellent stone for students and professionals.

Intuition and Insight: Celestobarite enhances intuitive abilities and spiritual insight. It opens the third eye and crown chakras, facilitating deeper connections to higher realms and spiritual guides.

Protection: Known for its protective properties, Celestobarite helps to shield the wearer from negative influences. It also has grounding properties that help individuals stay connected to their physical bodies and the Earth.

Physical Healing Properties

Nervous System Support: Celestobarite is believed to support the nervous system, enhancing its function and reducing stress and anxiety. It promotes overall mental well-being.

Detoxification: This gemstone aids in the detoxification process, supporting the body's natural ability to eliminate toxins. It enhances liver and kidney function, promoting overall metabolic health.

Immune System Boost: Celestobarite is thought to boost the immune system, helping the body to fight off infections and illnesses more effectively. It supports overall health and vitality.

Pain Relief: Celestobarite is known to provide relief from physical pain, particularly for conditions related to inflammation and muscle tension. It helps to reduce discomfort and promote overall physical well-being.

Cellular Regeneration: Celestobarite supports cellular regeneration and healing. It aids in the repair of tissues and can be beneficial in the recovery process from injuries and surgeries.

Potential Homeopathic Uses

If Celestobarite were to be used as a homeopathic remedy, its indications might include:

Psychological Symptoms: Mental fog, emotional instability, stress, and difficulty in spiritual connection.

Physical Symptoms: Nervous system support, detoxification needs, immune deficiencies, and pain relief.

Behavioral Symptoms: Challenges in maintaining focus, lack of emotional balance, and difficulties in managing stress.

Celestobarite's homeopathic profile would focus on its ability to heal, protect, and clarify, making it suitable for addressing conditions related to mental clarity, emotional healing, and overall vitality.

Conclusion

Celestobarite is a rare and powerful gemstone that offers a multitude of benefits for both physical and spiritual well-being. Its ability to enhance mental clarity, support emotional healing, and promote overall health makes it a valuable tool in holistic healing practices. Whether used in meditation, as a protective talisman, or for its physical healing properties, Celestobarite stands out as a gem of clarity and vitality. As with all alternative practices, these should complement conventional medical treatments and be used responsibly.

Cobaltite: Comprehensive Guide on Spiritual and Physical Healing Properties

Overview

Cobaltite is a rare mineral typically found in shades of silver-gray, with a metallic luster. This gemstone is highly valued for its unique energy, which is believed to promote mental clarity, emotional healing, and spiritual growth. Cobaltite is also known for its protective and grounding properties.

Spiritual and Psychic Benefits

Mental Clarity: Cobaltite is renowned for its ability to enhance mental clarity and focus. It helps to clear mental fog and improve concentration, making it an excellent stone for students and professionals.

Emotional Healing: This gemstone aids in emotional healing by helping to release negative emotions and past traumas. It promotes a sense of calm and emotional balance, making it easier to navigate life's challenges.

Spiritual Growth: Cobaltite enhances spiritual growth and insight. It helps individuals connect with their higher self and spiritual guides, facilitating deeper levels of understanding and awareness.

Protection: Known for its protective properties, Cobaltite helps to shield the wearer from negative influences. It also has grounding properties that help individuals stay connected to their physical bodies and the Earth.

Intuition and Insight: Cobaltite enhances intuitive abilities and spiritual insight. It opens the third eye and crown chakras, facilitating deeper connections to higher realms and spiritual guides.

Physical Healing Properties

Nervous System Support: Cobaltite is believed to support the nervous system, enhancing its function and reducing stress and anxiety. It promotes overall mental well-being.

Detoxification: This gemstone aids in the detoxification process, supporting the body's natural ability to eliminate toxins. It enhances liver and kidney function, promoting overall metabolic health.

Immune System Boost: Cobaltite is thought to boost the immune system, helping the body to fight off infections and illnesses more effectively. It supports overall health and vitality.

Pain Relief: Cobaltite is known to provide relief from physical pain, particularly for conditions related to inflammation and muscle tension. It helps to reduce discomfort and promote overall physical well-being.

Cellular Regeneration: Cobaltite supports cellular regeneration and healing. It aids in the repair of tissues and can be beneficial in the recovery process from injuries and surgeries.

Potential Homeopathic Uses

If Cobaltite were to be used as a homeopathic remedy, its indications might include:

Psychological Symptoms: Mental fog, emotional instability, stress, and difficulty in spiritual connection.

Physical Symptoms: Nervous system support, detoxification needs, immune deficiencies, and pain relief.

Behavioral Symptoms: Challenges in maintaining focus, lack of emotional balance, and difficulties in managing stress.

Cobaltite's homeopathic profile would focus on its ability to heal, protect, and clarify, making it suitable for addressing conditions related to mental clarity, emotional healing, and overall vitality.

Conclusion

Cobaltite is a rare and powerful gemstone that offers a multitude of benefits for both physical and spiritual well-being. Its ability to enhance mental clarity, support emotional healing, and promote overall health makes it a valuable tool in holistic healing practices. Whether used in meditation, as a protective talisman, or for its physical healing properties, Cobaltite stands out as a gem of clarity and vitality. As with all alternative practices, these should complement conventional medical treatments and be used responsibly.

Descloizite: Comprehensive Guide on Spiritual and Physical Healing Properties

Overview

Descloizite is a rare mineral typically found in colors ranging from brown to reddish-brown, with a metallic luster. This gemstone is highly valued for its unique energy, which is believed to promote mental clarity, emotional healing, and spiritual growth.

Spiritual and Psychic Benefits

Mental Clarity: Descloizite is renowned for its ability to enhance mental clarity and focus. It helps to clear mental fog and improve concentration, making it an excellent stone for students and professionals.

Emotional Healing: This gemstone aids in emotional healing by helping to release negative emotions and past traumas. It promotes a sense of calm and emotional balance, making it easier to navigate life's challenges.

Spiritual Growth: Descloizite enhances spiritual

growth and insight. It helps individuals connect with their higher self and spiritual guides, facilitating deeper levels of understanding and awareness.

Protection: Known for its protective properties, Descloizite helps to shield the wearer from negative influences. It also has grounding properties that help individuals stay connected to their physical bodies and the Earth.

Intuition and Insight: Descloizite enhances intuitive abilities and spiritual insight. It opens the third eye and crown chakras, facilitating deeper connections to higher realms and spiritual guides.

Physical Healing Properties

Nervous System Support: Descloizite is believed to support the nervous system, enhancing its function and reducing stress and anxiety. It promotes overall mental well-being.

Detoxification: This gemstone aids in the detoxification process, supporting the body's natural ability to eliminate toxins. It enhances liver and kidney function, promoting overall metabolic health.

Immune System Boost: Descloizite is thought to boost the immune system, helping the body to fight off infections and illnesses more effectively. It supports overall health and vitality.

Pain Relief: Descloizite is known to provide relief from physical pain, particularly for conditions related to inflammation and muscle tension. It helps to reduce discomfort and promote overall physical well-being.

Cellular Regeneration: Descloizite supports cellular regeneration and healing. It aids in the repair of tissues and can be beneficial in the recovery process from injuries and surgeries.

Potential Homeopathic Uses

If Descloizite were to be used as a homeopathic remedy, its indications might include:

Psychological Symptoms: Mental fog, emotional instability, stress, and difficulty in spiritual connection.

Physical Symptoms: Nervous system support, detoxification needs, immune deficiencies, and pain relief.

Behavioral Symptoms: Challenges in maintaining focus, lack of emotional balance, and difficulties in managing stress.

Descloizite's homeopathic profile would focus on its ability to heal, protect, and clarify, making it suitable for addressing conditions related to mental clarity, emotional healing, and overall vitality.

Conclusion

Descloizite is a rare and powerful gemstone that offers a multitude of benefits for both physical and spiritual well-being. Its ability to enhance mental clarity, support emotional healing, and promote overall health makes it a valuable tool in holistic healing practices. Whether used in meditation, as a protective talisman, or for its physical healing properties, Descloizite stands out as a gem of clarity and vitality. As with all alternative practices, these should complement conventional medical treatments and be used responsibly.

Bertrandite: Comprehensive Guide on Spiritual and Physical Healing Properties

Overview

Bertrandite is a rare mineral often associated with beryllium and is typically found in shades of white to pale yellow. This gemstone is highly valued for its unique energy, which is believed to promote mental clarity, emotional healing, and spiritual insight.

Spiritual and Psychic Benefits

Mental Clarity: Bertrandite is renowned for its ability to enhance mental clarity and focus. It helps to clear mental fog and improve concentration, making it an excellent stone for students and professionals.

Emotional Healing: This gemstone aids in emotional healing by helping to release negative emotions and past traumas. It promotes a sense of calm and emotional balance, making it easier to navigate life's challenges.

Spiritual Insight: Bertrandite enhances spiritual insight and intuition. It opens the third eye and crown chakras, facilitating deeper levels of understanding and awareness.

Intuition and Insight: Bertrandite enhances intuitive abilities and spiritual insight. It facilitates deeper connections to higher realms and spiritual guides.

Calming and Soothing: Known for its calming properties, Bertrandite helps to reduce stress and anxiety. It provides a soothing energy that helps to balance emotions and promote a sense of peace and relaxation.

Physical Healing Properties

Nervous System Support: Bertrandite is believed to support the nervous system, enhancing its function and reducing stress and anxiety. It promotes overall mental well-being.

Detox: This gemstone aids in the detoxification process, supporting the body's natural ability to eliminate toxins. It enhances liver and kidney function, promoting overall metabolic health.

Immune System Boost: Bertrandite is thought to boost the immune system, helping the body to fight off infections and illnesses more effectively. It supports overall health and vitality.

Pain Relief: Bertrandite is known to provide relief from physical pain, particularly for conditions related to inflammation and muscle tension. It helps to reduce discomfort and promote overall physical well-being.

Cellular Regeneration: Bertrandite supports cellular regeneration and healing. It aids in the repair of tissues and can be beneficial in the recovery process from injuries and surgeries.

Potential Homeopathic Uses

If Bertrandite were to be used as a homeopathic remedy, its indications might include:

Psychological Symptoms: Mental fog, emotional instability, stress, and difficulty in spiritual connection.

Physical Symptoms: Nervous system support, detoxification needs, immune deficiencies, and pain relief.

Behavioral Symptoms: Challenges in maintaining focus, lack of emotional balance, and difficulties in managing stress.

Bertrandite's homeopathic profile would focus on its ability to heal, protect, and clarify, making it suitable for addressing conditions related to mental clarity, emotional healing, and overall vitality.

Conclusion

Bertrandite is a rare and powerful gemstone that offers a multitude of benefits for both physical and spiritual well-being. Its ability to enhance mental clarity, support emotional healing, and promote overall health makes it a valuable tool in holistic healing practices. Whether used in meditation, as a calming talisman, or for its physical healing properties, Bertrandite stands out as a gem of clarity and vitality. As with all alternative practices, these should complement conventional medical treatments and be used responsibly.

Boji Stone: Comprehensive Guide on Spiritual and Physical Healing Properties

Overview

Boji Stone, also known as Kansas Pop Rock, is typically found in shades of brown and black and is known for its unique luster and texture. This gemstone is highly valued for its grounding energy and its ability to promote emotional healing, mental clarity, and spiritual insight.

Spiritual and Psychic Benefits

Grounding and Protection: Boji Stone is renowned for its strong grounding properties. It helps individuals stay connected to their physical bodies and the Earth, providing a sense of stability and security.

Emotional Healing: This gemstone aids in emotional healing by helping to release negative emotions and past traumas. It promotes a sense of calm and emotional balance, making it easier to navigate life's challenges.

Mental Clarity: Boji Stone enhances mental clarity and focus. It helps to clear mental fog and improve concentration, making it an excellent stone for students and professionals.

Intuition and Insight: Boji Stone enhances intuitive abilities and spiritual insight. It opens the third eye and crown chakras, facilitating deeper connections to higher realms and spiritual guides.

Energy Balance: Known for its ability to balance energy, Boji Stone helps to align the chakras and restore overall energetic equilibrium.

Physical Healing Properties

Nervous System Support: Boji Stone is believed to support the nervous system, enhancing its function and reducing stress and anxiety. It promotes overall mental well-being.

Detoxification: This gemstone aids in the detoxification process, supporting the body's natural ability to eliminate toxins. It enhances liver and kidney function, promoting overall metabolic health.

Immune System Boost: Boji Stone is thought to boost the immune system, helping the body to fight off infections and illnesses more effectively. It supports overall health and vitality.

Pain Relief: Boji Stone is known to provide relief from physical pain, particularly for conditions related to inflammation and muscle tension. It helps to reduce discomfort and promote overall physical well-being.

Cellular Regeneration: Boji Stone supports cellular regeneration and healing. It aids in the repair of tissues and can be beneficial in the recovery process from injuries and surgeries.

Potential Homeopathic Uses

If Boji Stone were to be used as a homeopathic remedy, its indications might include:

Psychological Symptoms: Emotional instability, stress, and difficulty in managing emotions.

Physical Symptoms: Nervous system support, detoxification needs, immune deficiencies, and pain relief.

Behavioral Symptoms: Challenges in maintaining focus, lack of emotional balance, and difficulties in managing stress.

Boji Stone's homeopathic profile would focus on its ability to heal, ground, and clarify, making it suitable for addressing conditions related to mental clarity, emotional healing, and overall vitality.

Conclusion

Boji Stone is a powerful gemstone that offers a multitude of benefits for both physical and spiritual well-being. Its ability to enhance mental clarity, support emotional healing, and promote overall health makes it a valuable tool in holistic healing practices. Whether used in meditation, as a protective talisman, or for its physical healing properties, Boji Stone stands out as a gem of clarity and vitality. As with all alternative practices, these should complement conventional medical treatments and be used responsibly.

Cacoxenite: Comprehensive Guide on Spiritual and Physical Healing Properties

Overview

Cacoxenite is a rare mineral often found as an inclusion in amethyst, displaying beautiful shades of golden-yellow to brown. This gemstone is highly valued for its unique energy, which is believed to promote spiritual growth, emotional healing, and mental clarity.

Spiritual and Psychic Benefits

Spiritual Growth: Cacoxenite is renowned for its ability to enhance spiritual growth and insight. It helps individuals connect with their higher self and spiritual guides, facilitating deeper levels of understanding and awareness.

Emotional Healing: This gemstone aids in emotional healing by helping to release negative emotions and past traumas. It promotes a sense of calm and emotional balance, making it easier to navigate life's challenges.

Mental Clarity: Cacoxenite enhances mental clarity and focus. It helps to clear mental fog and improve concentration, making it an excellent stone for students and professionals.

Intuition and Insight: Cacoxenite enhances intuitive abilities and spiritual insight. It opens the third eye and crown chakras, facilitating deeper connections to higher realms and spiritual guides.

Calming and Soothing: Known for its calming properties, Cacoxenite helps to reduce stress and anxiety. It provides a soothing energy that helps to balance emotions and promote a sense of peace and relaxation.

Physical Healing Properties

Immune System Boost: Cacoxenite is thought to boost the immune system, helping the body to fight off infections and illnesses more effectively. It supports overall health and vitality.

Detoxification: This gemstone aids in the detoxification process, supporting the body's natural ability to eliminate toxins. It enhances liver and kidney function, promoting overall metabolic health.

Pain Relief: Cacoxenite is known to provide relief from physical pain, particularly for conditions related to inflammation and muscle tension. It helps to reduce discomfort and promote overall physical well-being.

Cellular Regeneration: Cacoxenite supports cellular regeneration and healing. It aids in the repair of tissues and can be beneficial in the recovery process from injuries and surgeries.

Nervous System Support: Cacoxenite is believed to support the nervous system, enhancing its function and reducing stress and anxiety. It promotes overall mental well-being.

Potential Homeopathic Uses

If Cacoxenite were to be used as a homeopathic remedy, its indications might include:

Psychological Symptoms: Mental fog, emotional instability, stress, and difficulty in spiritual connection.

Physical Symptoms: Immune deficiencies, detoxification needs, pain relief, and nervous system support.

Behavioral Symptoms: Challenges in maintaining focus, lack of emotional balance, and difficulties in managing stress.

Cacoxenite's homeopathic profile would focus on its ability to heal, protect, and clarify, making it suitable for addressing conditions related to mental clarity, emotional healing, and overall vitality.

Conclusion

Cacoxenite is a rare and powerful gemstone that offers a multitude of benefits for both physical and spiritual well-being. Its ability to enhance mental clarity, support emotional healing, and promote overall health makes it a valuable tool in holistic healing practices. Whether used in meditation, as a calming talisman, or for its physical healing properties, Cacoxenite stands out as a gem of clarity and vitality. As with all alternative practices, these should complement conventional medical treatments and be used responsibly.

Chalcanthite: Comprehensive Guide on Spiritual and Physical Healing Properties

Overview

Chalcanthite is a striking mineral known for its vivid blue color and crystalline structure. This gemstone is highly valued for its unique energy, which is believed to promote spiritual growth, mental clarity, and emotional healing. Chalcanthite is also known for its powerful cleansing and protective properties.

Spiritual and Psychic Benefits

Spiritual Growth: Chalcanthite is renowned for its ability to enhance spiritual growth and insight. It helps individuals connect with their higher self and spiritual guides, facilitating deeper levels of understanding and awareness.

Mental Clarity: This gemstone enhances mental clarity and focus. It helps to clear mental fog and improve concentration, making it an excellent stone for students and professionals.

Emotional Healing: Chalcanthite aids in emotional healing by helping to release negative emotions and past traumas. It promotes a sense of calm and emotional balance, making it easier to navigate life's challenges.

Intuition and Insight: Chalcanthite enhances intuitive abilities and spiritual insight. It opens the third eye and crown chakras, facilitating deeper connections to higher realms and spiritual guides.

Cleansing and Protection: Known for its powerful cleansing properties, Chalcanthite helps to clear negative energy and protect the wearer from negative influences. It provides a strong energetic shield.

Physical Healing Properties

Detoxification: Chalcanthite aids in the detoxification process, supporting the body's natural ability to eliminate toxins. It enhances liver and kidney function, promoting overall metabolic health.

Pain Relief: Chalcanthite is known to provide relief from physical pain, particularly for conditions related to inflammation and muscle tension. It helps to reduce discomfort and promote overall physical well-being.

Immune System Boost: Chalcanthite is thought to boost the immune system, helping the body to fight off infections and illnesses more effectively. It supports overall health and vitality.

Cell Regeneration: Chalcanthite supports cellular regeneration and healing. It aids in the repair of tissues and can be beneficial in the recovery process from injuries and surgeries.

Nervous System Support: Chalcanthite is believed to support the nervous system, enhancing its function and reducing stress and anxiety. It promotes overall mental well-being.

Potential Homeopathic Uses

If Chalcanthite were to be used as a homeopathic remedy, its indications might include:

Psychological Symptoms: Mental fog, emotional instability, stress, and difficulty in spiritual connection.

Physical Symptoms: Detoxification needs, pain relief, immune deficiencies, and nervous system support.

Behavioral Symptoms: Challenges in maintaining focus, lack of emotional balance, and difficulties in managing stress.

Chalcanthite's homeopathic profile would focus on its ability to heal, cleanse, and protect, making it suitable for addressing conditions related to mental clarity, emotional healing, and overall vitality.

Conclusion

Chalcanthite is a powerful gemstone that offers a multitude of benefits for both physical and spiritual well-being. Its ability to enhance mental clarity, support emotional healing, and promote overall health makes it a valuable tool in holistic healing practices. Whether used in meditation, as a protective talisman, or for its physical healing properties, Chalcanthite stands out as a gem of clarity and vitality. As with all alternative practices, these should complement conventional medical treatments and be used responsibly.

Chiastolite: Comprehensive Guide on Spiritual and Physical Healing Properties

Overview

Chiastolite, also known as the "Cross Stone," is a unique variety of andalusite that typically exhibits a cross-shaped pattern in its structure. This gemstone is highly valued for its grounding energy and its ability to promote spiritual growth, mental clarity, and emotional healing.

Spiritual and Psychic Benefits

Spiritual Growth: Chiastolite is renowned for its ability to enhance spiritual growth and insight. It helps individuals connect with their higher self and spiritual guides, facilitating deeper levels of understanding and awareness.

Mental Clarity: This gemstone enhances mental clarity and focus. It helps to clear mental fog and improve concentration, making it an excellent stone for students and professionals.

Emotional Healing: Chiastolite aids in emotional healing by helping to release negative emotions and past traumas. It promotes a sense of calm and emotional balance, making it easier to navigate life's challenges.

Protection: Known for its strong protective properties, Chiastolite helps to shield the wearer from negative influences. It provides a sense of security and grounding.

Intuition and Insight: Chiastolite enhances intuitive abilities and spiritual insight. It opens the third eye and crown chakras, facilitating deeper connections to higher realms and spiritual guides.

Physical Healing Properties

Nervous System Support: Chiastolite is believed to support the nervous system, enhancing its function and reducing stress and anxiety. It promotes overall mental well-being.

Pain Relief: Chiastolite is known to provide relief from physical pain, particularly for conditions related to inflammation and muscle tension. It helps to reduce discomfort and promote overall physical well-being.

Immune System Boost: Chiastolite is thought to boost the immune system, helping the body to fight off infections and illnesses more effectively. It supports overall health and vitality.

Detoxification: This gemstone aids in the detoxification process, supporting the body's natural ability to eliminate toxins. It enhances liver and kidney function, promoting overall metabolic health.

Cellular Regeneration: Chiastolite supports cellular regeneration and healing. It aids in the repair of tissues and can be beneficial in the recovery process from injuries and surgeries.

Potential Homeopathic Uses

If Chiastolite were to be used as a homeopathic remedy, its indications might include:

Psychological Symptoms: Mental fog, emotional instability, stress, and difficulty in spiritual connection.

Physical Symptoms: Nervous system support, pain relief, immune deficiencies, and detoxification needs.

Behavioral Symptoms: Challenges in maintaining focus, lack of emotional balance, and difficulties in managing stress.

Chiastolite's homeopathic profile would focus on its ability to heal, protect, and ground, making it suitable for addressing conditions related to mental clarity, emotional healing, and overall vitality.

Conclusion

Chiastolite is a powerful gemstone that offers a multitude of benefits for both physical and spiritual well-being. Its ability to enhance mental clarity, support emotional healing, and promote overall health makes it a valuable tool in holistic healing practices. Whether used in meditation, as a protective talisman, or for its physical healing properties, Chiastolite stands out as a gem of clarity and vitality. As with all alternative practices, these should complement conventional medical treatments and be used responsibly.

Chlorastrolite (Greenstone): Comprehensive Guide on Spiritual and Physical Healing Properties

Overview

Chlorastrolite, also known as Greenstone, is a rare and beautiful mineral typically found in shades of green with a distinctive turtleback pattern. This gemstone is highly valued for its unique energy, which is believed to promote spiritual growth, emotional healing, and mental clarity.

Spiritual and Psychic Benefits

Spiritual Growth: Chlorastrolite is renowned for its ability to enhance spiritual growth and insight. It helps individuals connect with their higher self and spiritual guides, facilitating deeper levels of understanding and awareness.

Mental Clarity: This gemstone enhances mental clarity and focus. It helps to clear mental fog and improve concentration, making it an excellent stone for students and professionals.

Emotional Healing: Chlorastrolite aids in emotional healing by helping to release negative emotions and past traumas. It promotes a sense of calm and emotional balance, making it easier to navigate life's challenges.

Intuition and Insight: Chlorastrolite enhances intuitive abilities and spiritual insight. It opens the third eye and crown chakras, facilitating deeper connections to higher realms and spiritual guides.

Protection: Known for its strong protective properties, Chlorastrolite helps to shield the wearer from negative influences. It provides a sense of security and grounding.

Calming and Soothing: Known for its calming properties, Chlorastrolite helps to reduce stress and anxiety. It provides a soothing energy that helps to balance emotions and promote a sense of peace and relaxation.

Physical Healing Properties

Immune System Boost: Chlorastrolite is thought to boost the immune system, helping the body to fight off infections and illnesses more effectively. It supports overall health and vitality.

Detoxification: This gemstone aids in the detoxification process, supporting the body's natural ability to eliminate toxins. It enhances liver and kidney function, promoting overall metabolic health.

Pain Relief: Chlorastrolite is known to provide relief from physical pain, particularly for conditions related to inflammation and muscle tension. It helps to reduce discomfort and promote overall physical well-being.

Cellular Regeneration: Chlorastrolite supports cellular regeneration and healing. It aids in the repair of tissues and can be beneficial in the recovery process from injuries and surgeries.

Nervous System Support: Chlorastrolite is believed to support the nervous system, enhancing its function and reducing stress and anxiety. It promotes overall mental well-being.

Potential Homeopathic Uses

If Chlorastrolite were to be used as a homeopathic remedy, its indications might include:

Psychological Symptoms: Mental fog, emotional instability, stress, and difficulty in spiritual connection.

Physical Symptoms: Immune deficiencies, detoxification needs, pain relief, and nervous system support.

Behavioral Symptoms: Challenges in maintaining focus, lack of emotional balance, and difficulties in managing stress.

Chlorastrolite's homeopathic profile would focus on its ability to heal, protect, and clarify, making it suitable for addressing conditions related to mental clarity, emotional healing, and overall vitality.

Conclusion

Chlorastrolite is a rare and powerful gemstone that offers a multitude of benefits for both physical and spiritual well-being. Its ability to enhance mental clarity, support emotional healing, and promote overall health makes it a valuable tool in holistic healing practices. Whether used in meditation, as a calming talisman, or for its physical healing properties, Chlorastrolite stands out as a gem of clarity and vitality. As with all alternative practices, these should complement conventional medical treatments and be used responsibly.

Creedite: Comprehensive Guide on Spiritual and Physical Healing Properties

Overview

Creedite is a rare and beautiful mineral typically found in vibrant shades of orange, purple, or white. This gemstone is highly valued for its unique energy, which is believed to promote spiritual growth, emotional healing, and mental clarity. Creedite is also known for its ability to enhance communication and creativity.

Spiritual and Psychic Benefits

Spiritual Growth: Creedite is renowned for its ability to enhance spiritual growth and insight. It helps individuals connect with their higher self and spiritual guides, facilitating deeper levels of understanding and awareness.

Mental Clarity: This gemstone enhances mental clarity and focus. It helps to clear mental fog and improve concentration, making it an excellent stone for students and professionals.

Emotional Healing: Creedite aids in emotional healing by helping to release negative emotions and past traumas. It promotes a sense of calm and emotional balance, making it easier to navigate life's challenges.

Creativity and Communication: Creedite stimulates creativity and enhances communication skills. It is an excellent tool for artists, writers, and anyone involved in creative pursuits.

Intuition and Insight: Creedite enhances intuitive abilities and spiritual insight. It opens the third eye and crown chakras, facilitating deeper connections to higher realms and spiritual guides.

Physical Healing Properties

Nervous System Support: Creedite is believed to support the nervous system, enhancing its function and reducing stress and anxiety. It promotes overall mental well-being.

Pain Relief: Creedite is known to provide relief from physical pain, particularly for conditions related to inflammation and muscle tension. It helps to reduce discomfort and promote overall physical well-being.

Immune System Boost: Creedite is thought to boost the immune system, helping the body to fight off infections and illnesses more effectively. It supports overall health and vitality.

Detoxification: This gemstone aids in the detoxification process, supporting the body's natural ability to eliminate toxins. It enhances liver and kidney function, promoting overall metabolic health.

Cellular Regeneration: Creedite supports cellular regeneration and healing. It aids in the repair of tissues and can be beneficial in the recovery process from injuries and surgeries.

Potential Homeopathic Uses

If Creedite were to be used as a homeopathic remedy, its indications might include:

Psychological Symptoms: Mental fog, emotional instability, stress, and difficulty in communication.

Physical Symptoms: Nervous system support, pain relief, immune deficiencies, and detoxification needs.

Behavioral Symptoms: Challenges in maintaining focus, lack of emotional balance, and difficulties in managing stress.

Creedite's homeopathic profile would focus on its ability to heal, clarify, and inspire, making it suitable for addressing conditions related to mental clarity, emotional healing, and overall vitality.

Conclusion

Creedite is a powerful gemstone that offers a multitude of benefits for both physical and spiritual well-being. Its ability to enhance mental clarity, support emotional healing, and promote overall health makes it a valuable tool in holistic healing practices. Whether used in meditation, as a creative talisman, or for its physical healing properties, Creedite stands out as a gem of clarity and inspiration. As with all alternative practices, these should complement conventional medical treatments and be used responsibly.

Crocidolite: Comprehensive Guide on Spiritual and Physical Healing Properties

Overview

Crocidolite, commonly known as Blue Tiger's Eye or Hawk's Eye, is a striking mineral that exhibits beautiful chatoyant bands of blue and gray. This gemstone is renowned for its protective qualities and its ability to enhance intuition and inner strength. Crocidolite is primarily found in South Africa and Western Australia and is highly regarded for its ability to provide clarity and focus.

Spiritual and Psychic Benefits

Protection and Grounding: Crocidolite is celebrated for its strong protective properties. It serves as a shield against negative energies and psychic attacks, making it an excellent stone for empaths and those who are sensitive to external influences. Its grounding effect helps individuals stay anchored to the Earth, providing stability and balance.

Clarity and Focus: This gemstone is known to enhance mental clarity and focus. It aids in decision-making processes and helps to clear the mind of distractions, making it easier to concentrate on important tasks. Crocidolite is particularly beneficial for students and professionals who need to maintain high levels of concentration.

Intuition and Insight: Crocidolite opens the third eye chakra, enhancing intuitive abilities and spiritual insight. It helps individuals connect with their higher selves and access deeper levels of consciousness. This gemstone is ideal for those seeking to develop their psychic abilities and gain a clearer understanding of their spiritual path.

Emotional Stability: Crocidolite promotes emotional stability and balance. It helps to alleviate feelings of anxiety, stress, and fear, providing a sense of calm and security. This gemstone supports emotional resilience, making it easier to navigate challenging situations with grace and composure.

Courage and Strength: Known for its ability to boost inner strength and courage, Crocidolite empowers individuals to overcome fears and challenges. It encourages a positive outlook and helps to build self-confidence, making it easier to take bold steps towards one's goals.

Physical Healing Properties

Eye Health: Crocidolite is believed to support eye health and improve vision. It is often used to alleviate eye strain and support the healing of various eye conditions. This gemstone promotes overall ocular health and may help in maintaining sharp and clear vision.

Respiratory Health: This gemstone is known to support respiratory health, particularly in conditions related to asthma and bronchitis. It aids in the clearing of airways and helps to reduce inflammation, promoting easier breathing and overall respiratory well-being.

Nervous System Support: Crocidolite is known to support the nervous system, helping to alleviate symptoms of stress and anxiety. It promotes a sense of calm and relaxation, reducing the physical impact of stress on the body. This gemstone is beneficial for those who experience nervous tension and need support in calming their nerves.

Pain Relief: Crocidolite provides relief from physical pain, particularly in conditions related to inflammation and tension. It helps to reduce discomfort and promote overall physical well-being, making it a valuable tool for those dealing with chronic pain.

Detoxification: This gemstone aids in the detoxification process, supporting the body's natural ability to eliminate toxins. It enhances liver and kidney function, promoting overall metabolic health and efficient waste removal.

Potential Homeopathic Uses

If Crocidolite were to be used as a homeopathic remedy, its indications might include:

Psychological Symptoms: Anxiety, stress, emotional instability, and lack of clarity. It may also help with issues related to protection and grounding.

Physical Symptoms: Eye strain, respiratory conditions, nervous system support, and pain relief.

Behavioral Symptoms: Difficulty maintaining focus, managing stress, and overcoming fears.

Crocidolite's homeopathic profile would focus on its ability to protect, balance, and strengthen, making it suitable for addressing conditions related to stress, anxiety, and physical discomfort.

Conclusion

Crocidolite is a powerful gemstone that offers a multitude of benefits for both physical and spiritual well-being. Its ability to enhance mental clarity, support emotional stability, and promote overall health makes it a valuable tool in holistic healing practices. Whether used in meditation, as a protective talisman, or for its physical healing properties, Crocidolite stands out as a gem of clarity and strength. As with all alternative practices, these should complement conventional medical treatments and be used responsibly.

Gahnite: Comprehensive Guide on Spiritual and Physical Healing Properties

Overview

Gahnite, also known as zinc spinel, is a zinc aluminum oxide mineral that typically appears in shades of green, blue, and dark gray. This gemstone is known for its grounding and protective qualities and its ability to enhance personal strength and resilience. Gahnite is found in locations such as Sweden, Canada, and the United States.

Spiritual and Psychic Benefits

Grounding and Protection: Gahnite is celebrated for its strong grounding properties. It helps individuals stay connected to the Earth and their physical bodies, providing a sense of stability and security.

This grounding effect is particularly beneficial during meditation and spiritual practices.

Personal Strength: This gemstone is known to enhance personal strength and resilience. It supports individuals in overcoming challenges and building inner strength, making it easier to navigate difficult situations.

Emotional Stability: Gahnite promotes emotional stability and balance. It helps to alleviate feelings of anxiety, stress, and fear, providing a sense of calm and security. This gemstone supports emotional healing and resilience, making it easier to handle emotional challenges.

Intuition and Insight: Gahnite opens the third eye chakra, enhancing intuitive abilities and spiritual insight. It helps individuals connect with their higher selves and gain a deeper understanding of their life path. This gemstone is ideal for those seeking to develop their psychic abilities and access higher realms of consciousness.

Confidence and Courage: Known for its ability to boost confidence and courage, Gahnite empowers individuals to overcome fears and take bold steps towards their goals. It encourages a positive outlook and helps to build self-belief.

Physical Healing Properties

Immune System Support: Gahnite is believed to boost the immune system, enhancing the body's ability to fight off infections and illnesses. It supports overall health and vitality, promoting a strong and resilient immune response.

Pain Relief: This gemstone provides relief from physical pain, particularly in conditions related to inflammation and muscle tension. It helps to reduce discomfort and promote overall physical well-being.

Detoxification: Gahnite aids in the detoxification process, supporting the body's natural ability to eliminate toxins. It enhances liver and kidney function, promoting overall metabolic health and efficient waste removal.

Bone Health: Gahnite is known to support bone health and aid in the healing of fractures. It promotes the absorption of calcium and other essential minerals, making it beneficial for those who need to strengthen their skeletal system.

Stress Relief: Known for its calming properties, Gahnite helps to reduce stress and anxiety. It provides a soothing energy that helps to balance emotions and promote a sense of peace and well-being.

Potential Homeopathic Uses

If Gahnite were to be used as a homeopathic remedy, its indications might include:

Psychological Symptoms: Anxiety, stress, emotional instability, and lack of confidence. It may also help with issues related to grounding and protection.

Physical Symptoms: Immune system support, pain relief, detoxification, and bone health.

Behavioral Symptoms: Difficulty managing stress, lack of focus during calming tasks, and challenges in emotional balance.

Gahnite's homeopathic profile would focus on its ability to heal, balance, and energize, making it suitable for addressing conditions related to stress, energy depletion, and emotional instability.

Conclusion

Gahnite is a powerful gemstone that offers a multitude of benefits for both physical and spiritual well-being. Its ability to enhance mental clarity, support emotional healing, and promote overall health makes it a valuable tool in holistic healing practices. Whether used in meditation, as a grounding talisman, or for its physical healing properties, Gahnite stands out as a gem of stability and vitality. As with all alternative practices, these should complement conventional medical treatments and be used responsibly.

Hemimorphite: Comprehensive Guide on Spiritual and Physical Healing Properties

Overview

Hemimorphite is a beautiful blue to green mineral that is often found in botryoidal formations. This gemstone is highly valued for its calming and soothing energy, which is believed to promote emotional healing, spiritual growth, and mental clarity. Hemimorphite is known for its ability to enhance communication and foster a sense of inner peace.

Spiritual and Psychic Benefits

Spiritual Growth: Hemimorphite is renowned for its ability to enhance spiritual growth and insight. It helps individuals connect with their higher self and spiritual guides, facilitating deeper levels of understanding and awareness.

Mental Clarity: This gemstone enhances mental clarity and focus. It helps to clear mental fog and improve concentration, making it an excellent stone for students and professionals.

Emotional Healing: Hemimorphite aids in emotional healing by helping to release negative emotions and past traumas. It promotes a sense of calm and emotional balance, making it easier to navigate life's challenges.

Communication and Expression: Hemimorphite stimulates communication and enhances expression skills. It is an excellent tool for those who need to articulate their thoughts and feelings clearly and effectively.

Intuition and Insight: Hemimorphite enhances intuitive abilities and spiritual insight. It opens the third eye and crown chakras, facilitating deeper connections to higher realms and spiritual guides.

Physical Healing Properties

Nervous System Support: Hemimorphite is believed to support the nervous system, enhancing its function and reducing stress and anxiety. It promotes overall mental well-being.

Pain Relief: Hemimorphite is known to provide relief from physical pain, particularly for conditions related to inflammation and muscle tension. It helps to reduce discomfort and promote overall physical well-being.

Immune System Boost: Hemimorphite is thought to boost the immune system, helping the body to fight off infections and illnesses more effectively. It supports overall health and vitality.

Detoxification: This gemstone aids in the detoxification process, supporting the body's natural ability to eliminate toxins. It enhances liver and kidney function, promoting overall metabolic health.

Cellular Regeneration: Hemimorphite supports cellular regeneration and healing. It aids in the repair of tissues and can be beneficial in the recovery process from injuries and surgeries.

Potential Homeopathic Uses

If Hemimorphite were to be used as a homeopathic remedy, its indications might include:

Psychological Symptoms: Mental fog, emotional instability, stress, and difficulty in communication.

Physical Symptoms: Nervous system support, pain relief, immune deficiencies, and detoxification needs.

Behavioral Symptoms: Challenges in maintaining focus, lack of emotional balance, and difficulties in managing stress.

Hemimorphite's homeopathic profile would focus on its ability to heal, clarify, and calm, making it suitable for addressing conditions related to mental clarity, emotional healing, and overall vitality.

Conclusion

Hemimorphite is a powerful gemstone that offers a multitude of benefits for both physical and spiritual well-being. Its ability to enhance mental clarity, support emotional healing, and promote overall health makes it a valuable tool in holistic healing practices. Whether used in meditation, as a calming talisman, or for its physical healing properties, Hemimorphite stands out as a gem of clarity and peace. As with all alternative practices, these should complement conventional medical treatments and be used responsibly.

Chalcopyrite: Comprehensive Guide on Spiritual and Physical Healing Properties

Overview

Chalcopyrite, often referred to as Peacock Ore due to its vibrant iridescent colors, is a beautiful mineral with a metallic luster that ranges in hues from gold to blue and purple. This gemstone is renowned for its ability to foster new ideas and increase perception and insight. Chalcopyrite is primarily found in Peru, Australia, and the United States and is highly regarded for its ability to stimulate creativity and innovation.

Spiritual and Psychic Benefits

Transformation and Alignment: Chalcopyrite is celebrated for its transformative properties. It helps align one's energies with their higher purpose, facilitating personal growth and spiritual evolution. This gemstone is excellent for those undergoing significant life changes and seeking deeper alignment with their true selves.

Creativity and Innovation: This gemstone is known to enhance creativity and stimulate new ideas. It opens the mind to innovative thinking and helps individuals tap into their creative potential. Chalcopyrite is particularly beneficial for artists, writers, and anyone involved in creative pursuits.

Perception and Insight: Chalcopyrite enhances perception and insight, helping individuals see the true nature of situations and people. It aids in discerning the truth and provides clarity in complex situations. This gemstone is ideal for those seeking to develop their intuitive abilities and gain a deeper understanding of their surroundings.

Emotional Balance: Chalcopyrite promotes emotional balance and stability. It helps to alleviate feelings of anxiety, depression, and stress, providing a sense of peace and well-being. This gemstone supports emotional resilience, making it easier to navigate emotional challenges with grace and calm.

Courage and Confidence: Known for its ability to boost confidence and courage, Chalcopyrite empowers individuals to take bold steps towards their goals. It encourages a positive outlook and helps to build self-assurance, making it easier to overcome obstacles and challenges.

Physical Healing Properties

Immune System Support: Chalcopyrite is believed to support the immune system, helping the body to fight off infections and diseases. It promotes overall immune health and enhances the body's natural defenses.

Respiratory Health: This gemstone is known to support respiratory health, particularly in conditions related to colds, flu, and bronchitis. It aids in the clearing of airways and helps to reduce inflammation, promoting easier breathing and overall respiratory well-being.

Metabolic Health: Chalcopyrite is known to support metabolic health, helping to regulate the body's metabolic processes. It aids in digestion and supports the healthy functioning of the liver and kidneys.

Pain Relief: Chalcopyrite provides relief from physical pain, particularly in conditions related to inflammation and tension. It helps to reduce discomfort and promote overall physical well-being, making it a valuable tool for those dealing with chronic pain.

Detoxification: This gemstone aids in the detoxification process, supporting the body's natural ability to eliminate toxins. It enhances liver and kidney function, promoting overall metabolic health and efficient waste removal.

Potential Homeopathic Uses

If Chalcopyrite were to be used as a homeopathic remedy, its indications might include:

Psychological Symptoms: Anxiety, depression, emotional instability, and lack of clarity. It may also help with issues related to creativity and innovation.

Physical Symptoms: Immune system support, respiratory conditions, metabolic health, and pain relief.

Behavioral Symptoms: Difficulty maintaining focus, managing stress, and overcoming fears.

Chalcopyrite's homeopathic profile would focus on its ability to transform, balance, and strengthen, making it suitable for addressing conditions related to stress, anxiety, and physical discomfort.

Conclusion

Chalcopyrite is a powerful gemstone that offers a multitude of benefits for both physical and spiritual well-being. Its ability to enhance creativity, support emotional balance, and promote overall health makes it a valuable tool in holistic healing practices. Whether used in meditation, as a talisman, or for its physical healing properties, Chalcopyrite stands out as a gem of transformation and insight. As with all alternative practices, these should complement conventional medical treatments and be used responsibly.

Diopside: Comprehensive Guide on Spiritual and Physical Healing Properties

Overview

Diopside is a beautiful green gemstone that is known for its powerful healing properties and ability to connect individuals with the natural world. This gemstone is primarily found in the USA, Russia, and Finland. Diopside is revered for its capacity to promote emotional healing and enhance compassion.

Spiritual and Psychic Benefits

Emotional Healing: Diopside is celebrated for its ability to heal emotional wounds and trauma. It helps to release pent-up emotions and facilitates forgiveness and compassion. This gemstone is ideal for those looking to heal from past hurts and cultivate a more open heart.

Connection to Nature: Diopside enhances one's connection to the natural world. It promotes a sense of oneness with nature and helps individuals feel more grounded and in tune with the Earth. This gemstone is excellent for those who enjoy outdoor activities and seek to deepen their relationship with the environment.

Intuition and Insight: Diopside opens the heart chakra, enhancing intuitive abilities and spiritual insight. It helps individuals connect with their higher selves and access deeper levels of consciousness. This gemstone is ideal for those seeking to develop their psychic abilities and gain a clearer understanding of their spiritual path.

Calm and Tranquility: Diopside promotes a sense of calm and tranquility. It helps to alleviate feelings of anxiety, stress, and fear, providing a sense of peace and security. This gemstone supports emotional resilience, making it easier to navigate challenging situations with grace and composure.

Self-Love and Acceptance: Known for its ability to boost self-love and acceptance, Diopside empowers individuals to appreciate themselves and their unique qualities. It encourages a positive outlook and helps to build self-confidence, making it easier to embrace one's true self.

Physical Healing Properties

Bone Health: Diopside is believed to support bone health and promote the healing of fractures. It is often used to alleviate pain and support the recovery process in bone-related conditions.

Immune System Support: This gemstone is known to support the immune system, helping the body to fight off infections and diseases. It promotes overall immune health and enhances the body's natural defenses.

Detoxification: Diopside aids in the detoxification process, supporting the body's natural ability to eliminate toxins. It enhances liver and kidney function, promoting overall metabolic health and efficient waste removal.

Pain Relief: Diopside provides relief from physical pain, particularly in conditions related to inflammation and tension. It helps to reduce discomfort and promote overall physical well-being, making it a valuable tool for those dealing with chronic pain.

Heart Health: This gemstone is believed to support heart health, promoting overall cardiovascular well-being. It helps to reduce stress on the heart and supports healthy circulation.

Potential Homeopathic Uses

If Diopside were to be used as a homeopathic remedy, its indications might include:

Psychological Symptoms: Anxiety, stress, emotional instability, and lack of clarity. It may also help with issues related to self-love and acceptance.

Physical Symptoms: Bone health, immune system support, detoxification, and pain relief.

Behavioral Symptoms: Difficulty managing stress, overcoming fears, and fostering self-compassion.

Diopside's homeopathic profile would focus on its ability to heal, balance, and strengthen, making it suitable for addressing conditions related to stress, anxiety, and physical discomfort.

Conclusion

Diopside is a powerful gemstone that offers a multitude of benefits for both physical and spiritual well-being. Its ability to enhance emotional healing, support immune health, and promote overall well-being makes it a valuable tool in holistic healing practices. Whether used in meditation, as a talisman, or for its physical healing properties, Diopside stands out as a gem of compassion and tranquility. As with all alternative practices, these should complement conventional medical treatments and be used responsibly.

Spessartine: Comprehensive Guide on Spiritual and Physical Healing Properties

Overview

Spessartine, a variety of garnet known for its vibrant orange to reddish-orange color, is a striking gemstone that is highly valued for its energizing and empowering properties. This gemstone is primarily found in Brazil, Madagascar, and the USA. Spessartine is renowned for its ability to boost creativity and enhance personal power.

Spiritual and Psychic Benefits

Creativity and Inspiration: Spessartine is celebrated for its ability to stimulate creativity and inspiration. It opens the mind to new ideas and perspectives, making it easier to think outside the box. This gemstone is particularly beneficial for artists, writers, and anyone involved in creative pursuits.

Personal Power and Confidence: This gemstone is known to enhance personal power and boost self-confidence. It helps individuals recognize their inner strength and encourages them to take bold steps towards their goals. Spessartine is ideal for those seeking to build self-assurance and embrace their true potential.

Passion and Motivation: Spessartine enhances passion and motivation, providing the drive and determination needed to pursue one's dreams. It helps to ignite a sense of purpose and encourages a proactive approach to life. This gemstone is excellent for those who need a boost of energy and enthusiasm.

Emotional Healing: Spessartine promotes emotional healing and balance. It helps to alleviate feelings of sadness, fear, and emotional pain, providing a sense of joy and well-being. This gemstone supports emotional resilience, making it easier to navigate emotional challenges with grace and positivity.

Spiritual Growth: Known for its ability to facilitate spiritual growth, Spessartine helps individuals connect with their higher selves and access deeper levels of consciousness. It supports spiritual development and encourages a greater understanding of one's spiritual path.

Physical Healing Properties

Reproductive Health: Spessartine is believed to support reproductive health and improve fertility. It is often used to alleviate symptoms of hormonal imbalances and support overall reproductive well-being.

Metabolic Health: This gemstone is known to support metabolic health, helping to regulate the body's metabolic processes. It aids in digestion and supports the healthy functioning of the liver and kidneys.

Pain Relief: Spessartine provides relief from physical pain, particularly in conditions related to inflammation and tension. It helps to reduce discomfort and promote overall physical well-being, making it a valuable tool for those dealing with chronic pain.

Immune System Support: Spessartine is known to support the immune system, helping the body to fight off infections and diseases.

It promotes overall immune health and enhances the body's natural defenses.

Circulatory Health: This gemstone is believed to support circulatory health, promoting overall cardiovascular well-being. It helps to improve circulation and supports the healthy functioning of the heart.

Potential Homeopathic Uses

If Spessartine were to be used as a homeopathic remedy, its indications might include:

Psychological Symptoms: Sadness, fear, emotional instability, and lack of clarity. It may also help with issues related to creativity and personal power.

Physical Symptoms: Reproductive health, metabolic health, pain relief, and immune system support.

Behavioral Symptoms: Difficulty managing stress, overcoming fears, and fostering creativity.

Spessartine's homeopathic profile would focus on its ability to heal, balance, and energize, making it suitable for addressing conditions related to stress, anxiety, and physical discomfort.

Conclusion

Spessartine is a powerful gemstone that offers a multitude of benefits for both physical and spiritual well-being. Its ability to enhance creativity, support reproductive health, and promote overall well-being makes it a valuable tool in holistic healing practices. Whether used in meditation, as a talisman, or for its physical healing properties, Spessartine stands out as a gem of creativity and empowerment. As with all alternative practices, these should complement conventional medical treatments and be used responsibly.

Feldspar: Comprehensive Guide on Spiritual and Physical Healing Properties

Overview

Feldspar, a group of minerals that come in a variety of colors including white, pink, and green, is known for its abundance and versatile healing properties. This gemstone is primarily found in Italy, Turkey, and the USA. Feldspar is highly valued for its ability to promote self-awareness and enhance creativity.

Spiritual and Psychic Benefits

Self-Awareness and Reflection: Feldspar is celebrated for its ability to enhance self-awareness and reflection. It helps individuals understand their inner thoughts and emotions, promoting personal growth and self-discovery. This gemstone is ideal for those seeking to gain a deeper understanding of themselves and their motivations.

Creativity and Inspiration: This gemstone enhances creativity and inspiration, helping individuals tap into their artistic potential. It opens the mind to new ideas and perspectives, making it easier to think outside the box. Feldspar is particularly beneficial for artists, writers, and anyone involved in creative pursuits.

Intuition and Insight: Feldspar enhances intuition and insight, helping individuals see beyond the surface of situations and people. It aids in discerning the truth and provides clarity in complex situations. This gemstone is ideal for those seeking to develop their psychic abilities and gain a deeper understanding of their surroundings.

Emotional Balance: Feldspar promotes emotional balance and stability. It helps to alleviate feelings of anxiety, stress, and fear, providing a sense of peace and well-being. This gemstone supports emotional resilience, making it easier to navigate challenging situations with grace and composure.

Spiritual Growth: Known for its ability to facilitate spiritual growth, Feldspar helps individuals connect with their higher selves and access deeper levels of consciousness. It supports spiritual development and encourages a greater understanding of one's spiritual path.

Physical Healing Properties

Nervous System Support: Feldspar is known to support the nervous system, helping to alleviate symptoms of stress and anxiety. It promotes a sense of calm and relaxation, reducing the physical impact of stress on the body. This gemstone is beneficial for those who experience nervous tension and need support in calming their nerves.

Pain Relief: Feldspar provides relief from physical pain, particularly in conditions related to inflammation and tension. It helps to reduce discomfort and promote overall physical well-being, making it a valuable tool for those dealing with chronic pain.

Immune System Support: Feldspar is known to support the immune system

helping the body to fight off infections and diseases. It promotes overall immune health and enhances the body's natural defenses.

Detoxification: This gemstone aids in the detoxification process, supporting the body's natural ability to eliminate toxins. It enhances liver and kidney function, promoting overall metabolic health and efficient waste removal.

Skin Health: Feldspar is believed to support skin health, promoting overall dermatological well-being. It helps to alleviate skin-related issues and supports healthy skin regeneration.

Potential Homeopathic Uses

If Feldspar were to be used as a homeopathic remedy, its indications might include:

Psychological Symptoms: Anxiety, stress, emotional instability, and lack of clarity. It may also help with issues related to self-awareness and creativity.

Physical Symptoms: Nervous system support, pain relief, immune system support, and detoxification.

Behavioral Symptoms: Difficulty managing stress, overcoming fears, and enhancing creativity and inspiration.

Feldspar's homeopathic profile would focus on its ability to heal, balance, and support, making it suitable for addressing conditions related to stress, anxiety, and physical discomfort.

Conclusion

Feldspar is a versatile gemstone that offers a multitude of benefits for both physical and spiritual well-being. Its ability to enhance self-awareness, support nervous system health, and promote overall well-being makes it a valuable tool in holistic healing practices. Whether used in meditation, as a talisman, or for its physical healing properties, Feldspar stands out as a gem of creativity and reflection. As with all alternative practices, these should complement conventional medical treatments and be used responsibly.

Gypsum: Comprehensive Guide on Spiritual and Physical Healing Properties

Overview

Gypsum, a soft sulfate mineral often found in white or colorless crystal form, is known for its calming and soothing properties. This mineral is primarily found in Mexico, the USA, and Russia. Gypsum is highly valued for its ability to promote relaxation and support emotional healing.

Spiritual and Psychic Benefits

Calm and Relaxation: Gypsum is celebrated for its ability to promote calm and relaxation. It helps to alleviate feelings of anxiety, stress, and fear, providing a sense of peace and tranquility. This gemstone is ideal for those seeking to cultivate inner peace and reduce stress.

Emotional Healing: This gemstone enhances emotional healing and balance. It helps to release pent-up emotions and fosters forgiveness and compassion. Gypsum is particularly beneficial for those who need to heal from past traumas and cultivate emotional resilience.

Intuition and Insight: Gypsum enhances intuition and insight, helping individuals see beyond the surface of situations and people. It aids in discerning the truth and provides clarity in complex situations. This gemstone is ideal for those seeking to develop their psychic abilities and gain a deeper understanding of their surroundings.

Grounding and Stability: Gypsum promotes grounding and stability, helping individuals stay connected to the Earth. It provides a sense of security and balance, making it easier to navigate challenging situations with grace and composure. This gemstone is excellent for those who need to anchor their energies and remain focused.

Spiritual Growth: Known for its ability to facilitate spiritual growth, Gypsum helps individuals connect with their higher selves and access deeper levels of consciousness. It supports spiritual development and encourages a greater understanding of one's spiritual path.

Physical Healing Properties

Nervous System Support: Gypsum is known to support the nervous system, helping to alleviate symptoms of stress and anxiety. It promotes a sense of calm and relaxation, reducing the physical impact of stress on the body. This gemstone is beneficial for those who experience nervous tension and need support in calming their nerves.

Pain Relief: Gypsum provides relief from physical pain, particularly in conditions related to inflammation and tension. It helps to reduce discomfort and promote overall physical well-being, making it a valuable tool for those dealing with chronic pain.

Immune System Support: Gypsum is known to support the immune system, helping the body to fight off infections and diseases. It promotes overall immune health and enhances the body's natural defenses.

Detoxification: This gemstone aids in the detoxification process, supporting the body's natural ability to eliminate toxins. It enhances liver and kidney function, promoting overall metabolic health and efficient waste removal.

Bone Health: Gypsum is believed to support bone health and promote the healing of fractures. It is often used to alleviate pain and support the recovery process in bone-related conditions.

Potential Homeopathic Uses

If Gypsum were to be used as a homeopathic remedy, its indications might include:

Psychological Symptoms: Anxiety, stress, emotional instability, and lack of clarity. It may also help with issues related to calm and relaxation.

Physical Symptoms: Nervous system support, pain relief, immune system support, and detoxification.

Behavioral Symptoms: Difficulty managing stress, overcoming fears, and fostering emotional resilience.

Gypsum's homeopathic profile would focus on its ability to heal, balance, and support, making it suitable for addressing conditions related to stress, anxiety, and physical discomfort.

Conclusion

Gypsum is a gentle gemstone that offers a multitude of benefits for both physical and spiritual well-being. Its ability to promote relaxation, support nervous system health, and enhance overall well-being makes it a valuable tool in holistic healing practices. Whether used in meditation, as a talisman, or for its physical healing properties, Gypsum stands out as a gem of calm and healing. As with all alternative practices, these should complement conventional medical treatments and be used responsibly.

Halite: Comprehensive Guide on Spiritual and Physical Healing Properties

Overview

Halite, commonly known as rock salt, is a mineral that comes in various colors, including white, pink, and blue. This mineral is primarily found in the USA, Germany, and Poland. Halite is highly valued for its cleansing and purifying properties, both physically and spiritually.

Spiritual and Psychic Benefits

Cleansing and Purification: Halite is celebrated for its ability to cleanse and purify. It helps to clear negative energies from the aura and environment, promoting a sense of peace and well-being. This gemstone is ideal for those seeking to remove negative influences and create a more positive atmosphere.

Emotional Balance: This gemstone enhances emotional balance and stability. It helps to alleviate feelings of anxiety, stress, and fear, providing a sense of calm and security. Halite is particularly beneficial for those who need to stabilize their emotions and foster emotional resilience.

Intuition and Insight: Halite enhances intuition and insight, helping individuals see beyond the surface of situations and people. It aids in discerning the truth and provides clarity in complex situations. This gemstone is ideal for those seeking to develop their psychic abilities and gain a deeper understanding of their surroundings.

Grounding and Stability: Halite promotes grounding and stability, helping individuals stay connected to the Earth. It provides a sense of security and balance, making it easier to navigate challenging situations with grace and composure. This gemstone is excellent for those who need to anchor their energies and remain focused.

Spiritual Growth: Known for its ability to facilitate spiritual growth, Halite helps individuals connect with their higher selves and access deeper levels of consciousness. It supports spiritual development and encourages a greater understanding of one's spiritual path.

Physical Healing Properties

Detoxification: Halite aids in the detoxification process, supporting the body's natural ability to eliminate toxins. It enhances liver and kidney function, promoting overall metabolic health and efficient waste removal.

Immune System Support: Halite is known to support the immune system, helping the body to fight off infections and diseases. It promotes overall immune health and enhances the body's natural defenses.

Respiratory Health: Halite is known to support respiratory health, particularly in conditions related to asthma and bronchitis. It aids in the clearing of airways and helps to reduce inflammation, promoting easier breathing and overall respiratory well-being.

Skin Health: This gemstone is believed to support skin health, promoting overall dermatological well-being. It helps to alleviate skin-related issues and supports healthy skin regeneration.

Hydration and Electrolyte Balance: Halite is known for its ability to maintain hydration and electrolyte balance in the body. It supports overall fluid balance and helps to prevent dehydration.

Potential Homeopathic Uses

If Halite were to be used as a homeopathic remedy, its indications might include:

Psychological Symptoms: Anxiety, stress, emotional instability, and lack of clarity. It may also help with issues related to cleansing and purification.

Physical Symptoms: Detoxification, immune system support, respiratory health, and skin health.

Behavioral Symptoms: Difficulty managing stress, overcoming fears, and fostering emotional resilience.

Halite's homeopathic profile would focus on its ability to heal, balance, and purify, making it suitable for addressing conditions related to stress, anxiety, and physical discomfort.

Conclusion

Halite is a powerful gemstone that offers a multitude of benefits for both physical and spiritual well-being. Its ability to cleanse and purify, support immune health, and promote overall well-being makes it a valuable tool in holistic healing practices. Whether used in meditation, as a talisman, or for its physical healing properties, Halite stands out as a gem of purification and balance. As with all alternative practices, these should complement conventional medical treatments and be used responsibly.

Ilmenite: Comprehensive Guide on Spiritual and Physical Healing Properties

Overview

Ilmenite, a titanium-iron oxide mineral, is recognized for its metallic luster and often black or brownish-black color. This mineral is primarily found in Australia, Canada, and Norway. Ilmenite is valued for its grounding and stabilizing properties, making it a powerful tool for enhancing physical and emotional resilience.

Spiritual and Psychic Benefits

Grounding and Stability: Ilmenite is celebrated for its strong grounding properties. It helps individuals stay connected to the Earth, providing a sense of stability and balance. This gemstone is ideal for those who need to anchor their energies and remain focused during turbulent times.

Emotional Resilience: This gemstone enhances emotional resilience, helping individuals navigate through stress and adversity with greater ease. It fosters a sense of inner strength and stability, making it easier to cope with emotional challenges.

Intuition and Insight: Ilmenite enhances intuition and insight, helping individuals see beyond the surface of situations and people. It aids in discerning the truth and provides clarity in complex situations. This gemstone is perfect for those seeking to develop their psychic abilities and gain a deeper understanding of their surroundings.

Protection: Ilmenite offers protective qualities, shielding individuals from negative energies and environmental stressors. It is beneficial for those who are sensitive to external influences and need an energetic shield.

Physical Endurance: Known for its ability to boost physical endurance and strength, Ilmenite supports the body in maintaining energy levels and stamina. It encourages a proactive approach to physical well-being and resilience.

Physical Healing Properties

Immune System Support: Ilmenite is known to support the immune system, helping the body to fight off infections and diseases. It promotes overall immune health and enhances the body's natural defenses.

Detoxification: Ilmenite aids in the detoxification process, supporting the body's natural ability to eliminate toxins. It enhances liver and kidney function, promoting overall metabolic health and efficient waste removal.

Bone Health: This gemstone is believed to support bone health and promote the healing of fractures. It is often used to alleviate pain and support the recovery process in bone-related conditions.

Pain Relief: Ilmenite provides relief from physical pain, particularly in conditions related to inflammation and tension. It helps to reduce discomfort and promote overall physical well-being, making it a valuable tool for those dealing with chronic pain.

Circulatory Health: Ilmenite is known to support circulatory health, promoting overall cardiovascular well-being. It helps to improve circulation and supports the healthy functioning of the heart.

Potential Homeopathic Uses

If Ilmenite were to be used as a homeopathic remedy, its indications might include:

Psychological Symptoms: Anxiety, stress, emotional instability, and lack of clarity. It may also help with issues related to grounding and emotional resilience.

Physical Symptoms: Immune system support, detoxification, bone health, and pain relief.

Behavioral Symptoms: Difficulty managing stress, overcoming fears, and enhancing physical endurance.

Ilmenite's homeopathic profile would focus on its ability to heal, balance, and support, making it suitable for addressing conditions related to stress, anxiety, and physical discomfort.

Conclusion

Ilmenite is a powerful gemstone that offers a multitude of benefits for both physical and spiritual well-being. Its ability to enhance grounding, support immune health, and promote overall well-being makes it a valuable tool in holistic healing practices. Whether used in meditation, as a talisman, or for its physical healing properties, Ilmenite stands out as a gem of stability and resilience. As with all alternative practices, these should complement conventional medical treatments and be used responsibly.

Jamesonite: Comprehensive Guide on Spiritual and Physical Healing Properties

Overview

Jamesonite, a lead iron antimony sulfide mineral, is known for its dark metallic color and needle-like crystal formations. This mineral is primarily found in Mexico, Bolivia, and the USA. Jamesonite is valued for its protective and grounding properties, making it an essential tool for emotional and physical protection.

Spiritual and Psychic Benefits

Protection: Jamesonite is celebrated for its strong protective properties. It serves as a shield against negative energies and psychic attacks, making it an excellent stone for empaths and those who are sensitive to external influences. Its grounding effect helps individuals stay anchored to the Earth, providing stability and balance.

Grounding and Stability: This gemstone enhances grounding and stability, helping individuals stay connected to the Earth. It provides a sense of security and balance, making it easier to navigate challenging situations with grace and composure. Jamesonite is excellent for those who need to anchor their energies and remain focused.

Intuition and Insight: Jamesonite enhances intuition and insight, helping individuals see beyond the surface of situations and people. It aids in discerning the truth and provides clarity in complex situations. This gemstone is ideal for those seeking to develop their psychic abilities and gain a deeper understanding of their surroundings.

Emotional Balance: Jamesonite promotes emotional balance and stability. It helps to alleviate feelings of anxiety, stress, and fear, providing a sense of peace and well-being. This gemstone supports emotional resilience, making it easier to navigate emotional challenges with grace and calm.

Inner Strength: Known for its ability to boost inner strength and courage, Jamesonite empowers individuals to overcome fears and challenges. It encourages a positive outlook and helps to build self-confidence, making it easier to take bold steps towards one's goals.

Physical Healing Properties

Immune System Support: Jamesonite is known to support the immune system, helping the body to fight off infections and diseases. It promotes overall immune health and enhances the body's natural defenses.

Pain Relief: Jamesonite provides relief from physical pain, particularly in conditions related to inflammation and tension. It helps to reduce discomfort and promote overall physical well-being, making it a valuable tool for those dealing with chronic pain.

Detoxification: This gemstone aids in the detoxification process, supporting the body's natural ability to eliminate toxins. It enhances liver and kidney function, promoting overall metabolic health and efficient waste removal.

Nervous System Support: Jamesonite is known to support the nervous system, helping to alleviate symptoms of stress and anxiety. It promotes a sense of calm and relaxation, reducing the physical impact of stress on the body. This gemstone is beneficial for those who experience nervous tension and need support in calming their nerves.

Respiratory Health: This gemstone is believed to support respiratory health, particularly in conditions related to asthma and bronchitis. It aids in the clearing of airways and helps to reduce inflammation, promoting easier breathing and overall respiratory well-being.

Potential Homeopathic Uses

If Jamesonite were to be used as a homeopathic remedy, its indications might include:

Psychological Symptoms: Anxiety, stress, emotional instability, and lack of clarity. It may also help with issues related to protection and grounding.

Physical Symptoms: Immune system support, pain relief, detoxification, and nervous system support.

Behavioral Symptoms: Difficulty managing stress, overcoming fears, and enhancing emotional resilience.

Jamesonite's homeopathic profile would focus on its ability to heal, balance, and protect, making it suitable for addressing conditions related to stress, anxiety, and physical discomfort.

Conclusion

Jamesonite is a powerful gemstone that offers a multitude of benefits for both physical and spiritual well-being. Its ability to enhance protection, support immune health, and promote overall well-being makes it a valuable tool in holistic healing practices. Whether used in meditation, as a talisman, or for its physical healing properties, Jamesonite stands out as a gem of protection and stability. As with all alternative practices, these should complement conventional medical treatments and be used responsibly.

Kurnakovite: Comprehensive Guide on Spiritual and Physical Healing Properties

Overview

Kurnakovite, a rare borate mineral, is recognized for its clear to white crystal formations and powerful healing properties. This mineral is primarily found in Kazakhstan and the USA. Kurnakovite is highly valued for its ability to promote emotional healing and enhance spiritual growth.

Spiritual and Psychic Benefits

Emotional Healing: Kurnakovite is celebrated for its profound ability to heal emotional wounds and trauma. It helps release past emotional pain and fosters forgiveness and compassion. This gemstone is ideal for those seeking to heal from past hurts and cultivate a more open heart.

Spiritual Growth: This gemstone enhances spiritual growth and transformation. It helps individuals connect with their higher selves and access deeper levels of consciousness. Kurnakovite is perfect for those looking to expand their spiritual horizons and gain greater insight into their spiritual journey.

Intuition and Insight: Kurnakovite enhances intuition and insight, helping individuals see beyond the surface of situations and people. It aids in discerning the truth and provides clarity in complex situations. This gemstone is ideal for those seeking to develop their psychic abilities and gain a deeper understanding of their surroundings.

Calm and Tranquility: Kurnakovite promotes a sense of calm and tranquility. It helps to alleviate feelings of anxiety, stress, and fear, providing a sense of peace and security. This gemstone supports emotional resilience, making it easier to navigate challenging situations with grace and composure.

Courage and Confidence: Known for its ability to boost confidence and courage, Kurnakovite empowers individuals to take bold steps towards their goals. It encourages a positive outlook and helps build self-assurance, making it easier to overcome obstacles and challenges.

Physical Healing Properties

Immune System Support: Kurnakovite is known to support the immune system, helping the body to fight off infections and diseases. It promotes overall immune health and enhances the body's natural defenses.

Pain Relief: Kurnakovite provides relief from physical pain, particularly in conditions related to inflammation and tension. It helps to reduce discomfort and promote overall physical well-being, making it a valuable tool for those dealing with chronic pain.

Detoxification: This gemstone aids in the detoxification process, supporting the body's natural ability to eliminate toxins. It enhances liver and kidney function, promoting overall metabolic health and efficient waste removal.

Matlockite: Comprehensive Guide on Spiritual and Physical Healing Properties

Overview

Matlockite, a lead halide mineral, is noted for its yellow to greenish-yellow color and unique healing properties. Found primarily in England, this rare mineral is prized for its ability to enhance clarity of thought and provide protective energies.

Spiritual and Psychic Benefits

Clarity of Thought: Matlockite is celebrated for its ability to clear mental confusion and enhance logical thinking. It helps improve decision-making and problem-solving skills, making it ideal for those who need to think clearly under pressure.

Spiritual Protection: This gemstone provides strong protective energies, shielding individuals from negative influences and psychic attacks. It is particularly useful for those who feel vulnerable to external energies.

Enhanced Intuition: Matlockite boosts intuition and helps individuals trust their inner guidance. It aids in recognizing subtle cues and insights, enhancing one's overall perceptiveness.

Emotional Stability: Matlockite promotes emotional stability and resilience. It helps to balance mood swings and provides a sense of calm and composure, making it easier to manage stress and emotional turmoil.

Grounding and Centering: Known for its grounding properties, Matlockite helps individuals stay centered and connected to the earth. It is beneficial for those who feel scattered or disconnected from their physical environment.

Physical Healing Properties

Immune System Support: Matlockite is believed to support the immune system, helping the body to fight off infections and diseases. It promotes overall immune health and enhances the body's natural defenses.

Pain Relief: This gemstone provides relief from physical pain, particularly in conditions related to inflammation and tension. It helps to reduce discomfort and promote overall physical well-being.

Detoxification: Matlockite aids in the detoxification process, supporting the body's natural ability to eliminate toxins. It enhances liver and kidney function, promoting overall metabolic health and efficient waste removal.

Respiratory Health: This mineral supports respiratory health, helping to alleviate symptoms of lung-related conditions and improve overall lung function.

Bone Health: Matlockite is known to support bone health, helping to strengthen bones and prevent fractures. It is beneficial for those dealing with bone-related issues.

Potential Homeopathic Uses

If Matlockite were to be used as a homeopathic remedy, its indications might include:

Psychological Symptoms: Confusion, indecisiveness, and emotional instability. It may also help in cases of anxiety and stress.

Physical Symptoms: Immune system deficiencies, respiratory issues, and bone health support.

Behavioral Symptoms: Difficulty in managing stress, susceptibility to external influences, and a need for grounding.

Matlockite's homeopathic profile would focus on its ability to protect, clarify, and stabilize, making it suitable for addressing conditions related to mental clarity and physical resilience.

Conclusion

Matlockite is a powerful crystal in holistic healing, celebrated for its unique properties and protective energies. Whether used for mental clarity, emotional stability, or physical health, Matlockite serves as a potent aid in achieving overall well-being and harmony. As with all alternative practices, these should be considered as complementary to conventional medical treatments.

Queitite: Comprehensive Guide on Spiritual and Physical Healing Properties

Overview

Queitite, a rare mineral characterized by its white to colorless appearance, is esteemed for its exceptional healing qualities. Predominantly found in Italy, this mineral is treasured for its ability to enhance mental clarity and offer emotional support.

Spiritual and Psychic Benefits

Mental Clarity: Queitite is acclaimed for its capacity to dispel mental confusion and augment cognitive function. It improves focus, concentration, and memory.

Emotional Support: This gemstone provides robust emotional support, aiding individuals in processing and releasing negative emotions. It fosters a sense of calm and stability.

Spiritual Awareness: Queitite heightens spiritual awareness and enlightenment. It helps individuals connect with their inner wisdom and access higher levels of consciousness.

Intuition and Insight: Queitite amplifies intuition and insight, assisting individuals in comprehending the deeper meanings of life and experiences.

Protection: Known for its protective attributes, Queitite shields individuals from negative influences and emotional stress.

Physical Healing Properties

Immune System Support: Queitite is believed to enhance the immune system, aiding the body in combating infections and diseases.

Pain Relief: This gemstone alleviates physical pain, particularly in conditions associated with inflammation and tension.

Detoxification: Queitite supports the detoxification process, facilitating the body's natural ability to eliminate toxins.

Respiratory Health: Queitite enhances respiratory health, alleviating symptoms related to lung conditions.

Circulatory Health: Queitite promotes circulatory health by improving blood flow and reducing cardiovascular risks.

Potential Homeopathic Uses

If employed as a homeopathic remedy, Queitite's indications might encompass

Psychological Symptoms: Anxiety, emotional stress, and mental confusion.

Physical Symptoms: Immune system deficiencies, respiratory issues, and detoxification needs.

Behavioral Symptoms: Difficulty in managing stress, susceptibility to negative influences, and a need for emotional support.

Queitite's homeopathic profile would emphasize its clarifying, protective, and detoxifying abilities, making it suitable for addressing conditions related to mental and physical well-being.

Conclusion

Queitite is an indispensable crystal in holistic healing, revered for its unique properties and healing energies. Whether utilized for mental clarity, emotional support, or physical health, Queitite serves as a potent aid in achieving overall well-being and harmony. As with all alternative practices, these should be considered complementary to conventional medical treatments

Rutile: Comprehensive Guide on Spiritual and Physical Healing Properties

Overview

Rutile, a titanium dioxide mineral distinguished by its needle-like crystal formations, is celebrated for its potent healing attributes. Sourced from various locations worldwide, including Brazil and the USA, Rutile is esteemed for its capacity to foster spiritual growth and physical healing.

Spiritual and Psychic Benefits

Spiritual Growth: Rutile is renowned for its ability to stimulate spiritual development and transformation. It aids individuals in connecting with their higher selves and accessing deeper levels of consciousness.

Intuition and Insight: This gemstone enhances intuition and insight, enabling individuals to perceive the deeper meanings of life and experiences.

Emotional Healing: Rutile provides robust emotional healing, helping individuals process and release negative emotions. It nurtures a sense of calm and stability.

Protection: Known for its protective properties, Rutile shields individuals from negative influences and emotional stress.

Energy Amplification: Rutile is recognized for its ability to amplify energy, enhancing the effects of other healing crystals and personal energy.

Physical Healing Properties

Immune System Support: Rutile is believed to bolster the immune system, enhancing the body's defense mechanisms against infections and diseases.

Pain Relief: This gemstone offers relief from physical discomfort, particularly in conditions associated with inflammation and tension.

Detoxification: Rutile supports the detoxification process, aiding the body's natural ability to expel toxins.

Respiratory Health: Rutile enhances respiratory health, alleviating symptoms related to lung conditions.

Circulatory Health: Rutile supports circulatory health by improving blood flow and reducing the risk of cardiovascular issues.

Potential Homeopathic Uses

If employed as a homeopathic remedy, Rutile's indications might encompass

Psychological Symptoms: Anxiety, emotional stress, and mental confusion.

Physical Symptoms: Immune system deficiencies, respiratory issues, and detoxification needs.

Behavioral Symptoms: Difficulty in managing stress, vulnerability to negative influences, and a need for emotional support.

Rutile's homeopathic profile would emphasize its amplifying, protective, and detoxifying abilities, making it suitable for addressing conditions related to mental and physical well-being.

Conclusion

Rutile is an essential crystal in holistic healing, revered for its unique properties and therapeutic energies. Whether utilized for spiritual growth, emotional healing, or physical health, Rutile serves as a powerful aid in achieving overall well-being and harmony. As with all alternative practices, these should be considered complementary to conventional medical treatments

Sewardite: Comprehensive Guide on Spiritual and Physical Healing Properties

Overview

Sewardite, a rare arsenate mineral recognized by its reddish-brown to dark brown color, is treasured for its unique healing properties. Predominantly found in Mexico, this mineral is esteemed for its ability to enhance mental focus and provide emotional grounding.

Spiritual and Psychic Benefits

Mental Focus: Sewardite is celebrated for its ability to improve mental clarity and concentration. It enhances cognitive function, making it ideal for those who require mental sharpness.

Emotional Grounding: This gemstone offers robust emotional grounding, helping individuals remain balanced and centered. It is particularly beneficial for those overwhelmed by their emotions.

Spiritual Awareness: Sewardite heightens spiritual awareness and assists individuals in connecting with their inner selves. It supports deepening one's spiritual practice and understanding.

Protection: Known for its protective properties, Sewardite shields individuals from negative energies and emotional stress. It fosters a safe and harmonious environment.

Stability and Balance: Sewardite promotes stability and balance in all aspects of life. It aligns the chakras and stabilizes the mood, fostering a sense of well-being and tranquility.

Physical Healing Properties

Immune System Support: Sewardite is believed to bolster the immune system, enhancing the body's defense mechanisms against infections and diseases.

Pain Relief: This gemstone alleviates physical discomfort, particularly in conditions associated with inflammation and tension.

Detoxification: Sewardite supports the detoxification process, aiding the body's natural ability to expel toxins. It enhances liver and kidney function, promoting metabolic health and efficient waste removal.

Respiratory Health: Sewardite enhances respiratory health, alleviating symptoms related to lung conditions and improving overall lung function.

Circulatory Health: Sewardite promotes circulatory health by improving blood flow and reducing the risk of cardiovascular issues. It helps maintain a healthy heart and vascular system.

Potential Homeopathic Uses

If employed as a homeopathic remedy, Sewardite's indications might encompass

Psychological Symptoms: Anxiety, emotional stress, and mental confusion. It may also assist with emotional detachment and isolation.

Physical Symptoms: Immune system deficiencies, respiratory issues, and detoxification needs.

Behavioral Symptoms: Difficulty in managing stress, vulnerability to negative influences, and a need for emotional grounding.

Sewardite's home opathic profile would emphasize its focusing, protective, and detoxifying abilities, making it suitable for addressing conditions related to mental and physical well-being.

Conclusion

Sewardite is a powerful crystal in holistic healing, revered for its unique properties and grounding energies. Whether utilized for mental focus, emotional grounding, or physical health, Sewardite serves as a potent aid in achieving overall well-being and harmony. As with all alternative practices, these should be considered complementary to conventional medical treatments

Topazolite: Comprehensive Guide on Spiritual and Physical Healing Properties

Overview

Topazolite, a variety of andradite garnet, is esteemed for its yellow-green to green hues and potent healing attributes. Found in various locations worldwide, including Italy and the USA, Topazolite is treasured for its ability to promote mental clarity and enhance emotional well-being.

Spiritual and Psychic Benefits

Mental Clarity: Topazolite is celebrated for its capacity to dispel mental fog and enhance cognitive function. It improves focus, concentration, and memory.

Emotional Healing: This gemstone provides robust emotional healing, aiding individuals in processing and releasing negative emotions. It fosters a sense of calm and stability.

Spiritual Awareness: Topazolite heightens spiritual awareness and enlightenment. It helps individuals connect with their inner wisdom and access higher levels of consciousness.

Protection: Known for its protective properties, Topazolite shields individuals from negative influences and emotional stress. It creates a safe and harmonious environment.

Energy Amplification: Topazolite is recognized for its ability to amplify energy, enhancing the effects of other healing crystals and personal energy.

Physical Healing Properties

Immune System Support: Topazolite is believed to bolster the immune system, enhancing the body's defense mechanisms against infections and diseases.

Pain Relief: This gemstone offers relief from physical discomfort, particularly in conditions associated with inflammation and tension.

Detoxification: Topazolite supports the detoxification process, aiding the body's natural ability to expel toxins. It enhances liver and kidney function, promoting metabolic health and efficient waste removal.

Respiratory Health: Topazolite enhances respiratory health, alleviating symptoms related to lung conditions.

Circulatory Health: Topazolite promotes circulatory health by improving blood flow and reducing cardiovascular risks.

Potential Homeopathic Uses

If employed as a homeopathic remedy, Topazolite's indications might encompass

Psychological Symptoms: Anxiety, emotional stress, and mental confusion. It may also assist with emotional detachment and isolation.

Physical Symptoms: Immune system deficiencies, respiratory issues, and detoxification needs.

Behavioral Symptoms: Difficulty in managing stress, susceptibility to negative influences, and a need for emotional healing.

Topazolite's homeopathic profile would emphasize its clarifying, protective, and detoxifying abilities, making it suitable for addressing conditions related to mental and physical well-being.

Conclusion

Topazolite is an indispensable crystal in holistic healing, revered for its unique properties and therapeutic energies. Whether utilized for mental clarity, emotional healing, or physical health, Topazolite serves as a powerful aid in achieving overall well-being and harmony. As with all alternative practices, these should be considered complementary to conventional medical treatments

Ulvospinel: Comprehensive Guide on Spiritual and Physical Healing Properties

Overview

Ulvospinel, a member of the spinel group distinguished by its black to brownish-black color and magnetic properties, is treasured for its unique healing attributes. Predominantly sourced from Norway and the USA, this mineral is esteemed for its ability to enhance grounding and provide protective energies.

Spiritual and Psychic Benefits

Grounding: Ulvospinel is celebrated for its ability to ground individuals, helping them stay connected to the earth. It is particularly useful for those who feel scattered or disconnected from their physical environment.

Protection: This gemstone offers robust protective energies, shielding individuals from negative influences and emotional stress. It fosters a safe and harmonious environment.

Emotional Stability: Ulvospinel promotes emotional stability and resilience. It helps balance mood swings and provides a sense of calm and composure, facilitating stress management.

Spiritual Awareness: Ulvospinel heightens spiritual awareness and assists individuals in connecting with their inner selves. It supports deepening one's spiritual practice and understanding.

Energy Regulation: Known for its magnetic properties, Ulvospinel aids in regulating and balancing personal energy. It enhances the body's natural energy flow, promoting overall well-being.

Physical Healing Properties

Immune System Support: Ulvospinel is believed to bolster the immune system, enhancing the body's defense mechanisms against infections and diseases.

Pain Relief: This gemstone alleviates physical discomfort, particularly in conditions associated with inflammation and tension.

Detoxification: Ulvospinel supports the detoxification process, aiding the body's natural ability to expel toxins. It enhances liver and kidney function, promoting metabolic health and efficient waste removal.

Respiratory Health: Ulvospinel enhances respiratory health, alleviating symptoms related to lung conditions.

Circulatory Health: Ulvospinel promotes circulatory health by improving blood flow and reducing cardiovascular risks.

Potential Homeopathic Uses

If employed as a homeopathic remedy, Ulvospinel's indications might encompass

Psychological Symptoms: Anxiety, emotional stress, and mental confusion. It may also assist with emotional detachment and isolation.

Physical Symptoms: Immune system deficiencies, respiratory issues, and detoxification needs.

Behavioral Symptoms: Difficulty in managing stress, vulnerability to negative influences, and a need for grounding.

Ulvospinel's homeopathic profile would emphasize its grounding, protective, and detoxifying abilities, making it suitable for addressing conditions related to mental and physical well-being.

Conclusion

Ulvospinel is a powerful crystal in holistic healing, revered for its unique properties and grounding energies. Whether utilized for grounding, emotional stability, or physical health, Ulvospinel serves as a potent aid in achieving overall well-being and harmony. As with all alternative practices, these should be considered complementary to conventional medical treatments

Veszelyite: Comprehensive Guide on Spiritual and Physical Healing Properties

Overview

Veszelyite, a rare phosphate mineral, is distinguished by its bright blue to green coloration and potent healing attributes. Predominantly sourced from the USA and Chile, this mineral is esteemed for its capacity to promote emotional recovery and stimulate spiritual advancement.

Spiritual and Psychic Benefits

Emotional Healing: Veszelyite is celebrated for its profound ability to mend emotional scars and trauma. It facilitates the release of past emotional pain and nurtures forgiveness and compassion.

Spiritual Growth: This gemstone augments spiritual development and metamorphosis. It aids individuals in connecting with their higher selves and accessing deeper realms of consciousness.

Intuition and Insight: Veszelyite sharpens intuition and insight, enabling individuals to perceive beyond the superficial aspects of situations and people. It assists in discerning the truth and provides clarity in intricate circumstances.

Calm and Tranquility: Veszelyite induces a state of calm and tranquility. It alleviates anxiety, stress, and fear, imparting a sense of peace and security.

Courage and Confidence: Esteemed for its ability to bolster confidence and courage, Veszelyite empowers individuals to undertake bold strides towards their aspirations. It fosters a positive outlook and helps build self-assurance.

Physical Healing Properties

Immune System Support: Veszelyite is believed to bolster the immune system, enhancing the body's defense mechanisms against infections and diseases. It promotes overall immune health.

Pain Relief: Veszelyite offers relief from physical discomfort, particularly in conditions associated with inflammation and tension.

Detoxification: This gemstone aids in the detoxification process, supporting the body's natural ability to expel toxins. It enhances liver and kidney function, promoting metabolic health and efficient waste removal.

Respiratory Health: Veszelyite supports respiratory health, alleviating symptoms related to lung conditions and improving overall lung function.

Circulatory Health: Veszelyite promotes circulatory health by improving blood flow and reducing the risk of cardiovascular issues. It helps maintain a healthy heart and vascular system.

Potential Homeopathic Uses

If employed as a homeopathic remedy, Veszelyite's indications might encompass

Psychological Symptoms: Anxiety, emotional stress, and trauma. It may also assist with emotional detachment and isolation.

Physical Symptoms: Immune system deficiencies, respiratory issues, and detoxification requirements.

Behavioral Symptoms: Difficulty in managing stress, vulnerability to negative influences, and a need for courage and confidence.

Veszelyite's homeopathic profile would emphasize its healing, protective, and detoxifying abilities, making it suitable for addressing conditions related to emotional and physical well-being.

Conclusion

Veszelyite is an essential crystal in holistic healing, revered for its unique properties and therapeutic energies. Whether utilized for emotional healing, spiritual growth, or physical health, Veszelyite serves as a powerful aid in achieving overall well-being and harmony. As with all alternative practices, these should be considered complementary to conventional medical treatments

Chapter Summary

This chapter offers an extensive exploration into the spiritual, emotional, and physical healing properties of unique gemstones. It is designed to provide a holistic understanding of how these gemstones can be utilized within homeopathic and alternative healing practices to promote overall well-being.

At the heart of gemstone homeopathy is the belief in the interconnectedness of the mind, body, and spirit. Each gemstone possesses unique vibrational frequencies that resonate with different aspects of human health. By leveraging these frequencies, practitioners aim to restore balance and harmony, addressing not only physical ailments but also emotional and spiritual imbalances. This approach recognizes that true healing encompasses all dimensions of the self, leading to a more profound and lasting well-being.

Many of the gemstones covered in this chapter are renowned for their ability to enhance spiritual growth and psychic abilities. Stones like Amethyst, Selenite, and Lapis Lazuli are highlighted for their capacity to open the third eye and crown chakras, facilitating deeper meditation, intuition, and spiritual awareness. These gemstones serve as powerful tools for those seeking to deepen their spiritual practice and connect with higher realms of consciousness. The chapter also explores how gemstones like Moldavite and Celestite can assist in astral travel and communication with spirit guides.

Emotional well-being is a significant focus in the Materia Medica. Gemstones such as Rose Quartz, Rhodochrosite, and Lepidolite are celebrated for their soothing and nurturing energies. They help release emotional blockages, heal past traumas, and foster a sense of love, compassion, and inner peace. The chapter provides detailed insights into how these stones can be used to support emotional healing and stability. Additionally, it discusses the role of gemstones like Moonstone and Amazonite in balancing emotional states and promoting a calm, harmonious disposition.

Protection is a recurring theme throughout the chapter. Gemstones like Black Tourmaline, Hematite, and Smoky Quartz are known for their strong protective properties. They act as energetic shields, safeguarding the user from negative influences, psychic attacks, and electromagnetic pollution. The chapter elaborates on how these stones can be used to create a safe and secure environment for spiritual practices. Furthermore, it examines the protective roles of Obsidian and Shungite, which are particularly effective in grounding and detoxifying energies.

The physical healing attributes of gemstones are thoroughly explored. Stones such as Bloodstone, Carnelian, and Malachite are recognized for their ability to enhance vitality, support the immune system, and promote physical regeneration.

The chapter offers comprehensive information on how these gemstones can aid in the recovery from illnesses, alleviate pain, and support overall physical health. It also covers how gemstones like Amber and Chrysocolla can aid in detoxification processes and improve respiratory health, providing a holistic approach to physical wellness.

Detoxification is another critical aspect covered in the Materia Medica. Gemstones like Fluorite, Apatite, and Chrysoprase are noted for their cleansing properties. They assist in purifying the body, mind, and spirit from toxins and negative energies. The chapter provides guidance on using these stones to support detoxification processes and maintain energetic purity. Additionally, it discusses the use of gemstones like Clear Quartz and Citrine in amplifying and focusing cleansing energies, making them indispensable tools in purification rituals.

The chapter emphasizes the importance of chakra balancing in holistic healing. Each gemstone is associated with specific chakras, helping to align and balance the body's energy centers. For example, Citrine is linked to the solar plexus chakra, promoting confidence and personal power, while Aquamarine resonates with the throat chakra, enhancing communication and self-expression. The Materia Medica offers detailed instructions on using gemstones for chakra healing and alignment, including practical layouts and meditations for optimal energy flow.

Many gemstones are known for their ability to amplify energy, enhancing the effects of other healing practices. Clear Quartz, for instance, is often referred to as the "master healer" for its capacity to amplify the energy of other stones and intentions. The chapter delves into how these amplifying stones can be incorporated into healing rituals to boost their effectiveness. It also explores the synergistic effects of combining gemstones, such as using Amethyst and Rose Quartz together to enhance spiritual and emotional healing.

Each gemstone in the chapter is presented with a detailed homeopathic profile, outlining its psychological, physical, and behavioral indications. This includes descriptions of the symptoms and conditions that the gemstone can address, providing a practical guide for practitioners to select the appropriate stone for their needs. The profiles also highlight the unique energetic signatures of each gemstone, offering a deeper understanding of their healing potential. Special attention is given to rare and powerful gemstones like Phenacite and Larimar, which possess exceptional healing properties.

The chapter concludes with practical advice on incorporating gemstone remedies into daily life. This includes methods for wearing gemstones as jewelry, using them in meditation, placing them in living spaces, and creating gemstone elixirs. The guidance provided ensures that readers can effectively harness the healing properties of gemstones to enhance their well-being. Additionally, the chapter covers advanced techniques such as using gemstone grids for energy work and integrating gemstones into holistic therapies like Reiki and acupuncture.

In summary, the chapter on Materia Medica of gemstone homeopathic remedies is a comprehensive resource that encapsulates the profound healing potential of these unique gemstones. It offers valuable insights into the spiritual, emotional, and physical benefits of gemstones, empowering readers to integrate these powerful tools into their holistic healing practices. This chapter serves as an essential guide for anyone interested in exploring the transformative power of gemstones and their applications in achieving overall well-being.

I hope you enjoyed this book entitled volume two. There are several more volumes on this particular topic which follow.

If you have any questions, please feel free
to write me at:

drvictordenispurcell@proton.me

Also by Dr Víctor Denis Purcell

2
Materia Medica of Homeopathic Gemstones

Standalone
Zen and the Way of the Artist
Zen and the Art of Medicine
Zen and the Way of the Artist
The Yoga Book
Zen and the Art of Living and Dying
Zen and the Art of Photography
The Homeopathic Book
das homöopathische buch
El Libro De Homeopatía
Le Livre Homéopathique
The Traveler's Handbook
❖❖❖❖❖❖❖❖❖❖
"Architectural and Interior Design Mastery: A Global Perspective"
Medicinal Mushrooms
The New Testament
"Das Neue Testament, 2024"
Новый Завет
Mini Materia Medica

The Receptive Warrior
The God Center
The American Constitution
A Deep Dive Into Death
The Voyager's Odyssey
Mini Materia Medica
Mini Materia Medica
Spiritual Medicine: Materia Medica of Homeopathic Gemstones and Crystals
Spirituelle Medizin: Materia Medica der homöopathischen Edelsteine und Kristalle
Materia Medica of Homeopathic Gemstones
Médecine spirituelle Materia Medica des gemmes et cristaux homéopathiques
Materia Medica of Homeopathic Gemstones
Volume Two: Materia Medica of Homeopathic Gemstones
Volume Three: Materia Materia of Homeopathic Gemstones

About the Author

Victor Denis Purcell is a certified homeopathic practitioner with a master's degree in educational psychology. With a deep-rooted passion for homeopathic medicine, he has been actively involved in this field since 1982. Over the decades, he has authored numerous books covering a wide range of topics, demonstrating a profound understanding and expertise in homeopathic practices and holistic healing. Through a combination of professional experience and scholarly dedication, Victor Denis Purcell continues to contribute significantly to the advancement and awareness of homeopathic medicine.